CAREERS IN
SPORT
Louise Fyfe

Fourth Edition

First published in 1983, author Chris Middleton
Second edition 1987, author Chris Middleton
Third edition 1990, authors Louise Fyfe and Andrew Shields
Fourth edition 1992, author Louise Fyfe

Kogan Page Limited
120 Pentonville Road
London N1 9JN

© Kogan Page 1983, 1987, 1990, 1992

British Library Cataloguing in Publication Data

A CIP record for this book is available from the British Library.

ISBN 0 7494 0806 5

Typeset by DP Photosetting, Aylesbury, Bucks
Printed and bound in Great Britain by
Clays Ltd, St Ives plc

Contents

Part 2

Introduction

If you asked a group of people about their dreams in life, you can be sure that many of their fantasies would have a sporting connection. After all, who hasn't at some time imagined what it would be like to score the winning goal in a Wembley Cup Final, to hit the shot that clinches a Wimbledon title, or to hole the final putt in a major golf championship?

It's little wonder that we all have dreams like these because sport plays such a major part in our lives. Even if they have never been to a football ground in years, people have their own 'pet' teams whose results they look for each Saturday. And in the summer, Test Matches and tennis become topics of conversation among people who would not normally be seen reading the sports pages of the newspapers.

The sportsmen and women who figure in these dreams are, in many cases, national heroes and heroines. Some of them earn large amounts of money, appear regularly on television, and command a lifestyle that is the envy of lesser mortals. The thought that all this is possible simply from playing a game that one loves is very attractive.

However, for every famous footballer or show-jumper, golfer or racing driver, there are literally thousands who have striven to get to the top and failed. Some have been cruelly unlucky when on the verge of success, maybe suffering a serious injury which ended their career before it had really begun. Others have progressed some way up the ladder, then realised for themselves or been told by a coach or manager that they would never climb much further. And then there are the millions of ordinary folk who would have loved the chance but are now perfectly happy to restrict their daydreams to the local tennis courts or cricket field.

Yet, for the few who are skilled, dedicated and fortunate enough, there *are* ways to make all these fantasies come true. Even though the wrong bounce of a ball, twist of an ankle or missing of a shot can leave a career in tatters, such risks are all part and parcel of earning a living from playing sport. The aim of this book is to highlight the recognised paths down which the determined can travel in order to achieve their goal.

The Leisure Profession

A career in sport does not have to be solely about playing. In the last decade, a profession based around 'leisure' has developed which offers the chance to work in sport to far more people than does simply playing.

'Leisure' is a word which has taken on a new meaning in recent years. In the past, it simply meant freedom from work, and described all those hours we might spend outside the classroom, the office or the factory. Now, leisure suggests something that is organised for us to do in our free time – and if something is organised, then of course it needs people to do the organising! It could be that one person will choose to spend his or her leisure time having a gentle swim at a nearby sports centre. Another might opt to pass the day in a country park. Yet another might wish to spend a few hours enjoying the attractions of a theme park. All of these come under the broad heading of leisure, and require people with a very wide range of skills and interests to manage and organise them.

Sport is now only a part of the leisure industry, but it is a booming part. Many of those men and women mentioned earlier who dream of playing at Lord's or Wimbledon take part regularly in amateur or 'recreational' sport. There are thousands of recognised clubs all over Britain, catering for everything from archery to yoga, badminton to ballooning. In addition, there are all those people who enjoy individual sports like angling or rifle shooting, the Sunday morning footballers who play in the local park, and the office netball teams and squash ladders. What is more, these people don't only enjoy their sport at weekends; with retirement ages falling, increased unemployment, more annual holiday and a much greater awareness of the importance of good health and fitness, sport is a seven-days-a-week business.

In order to cater for all these participants, new facilities have to be provided. The Sports Council, the government-funded organisation which helps to do this, estimates that more than 500 sports halls and 200 swimming pools need to be built just to cope with the current demand. A number of private companies are also realising that leisure is a growth industry and are putting their money into major developments in order to make a profit. But whether private sector or public, sports hall, squash club or swimming pool, people are needed to supervise and manage both the facilities and the activities taking place in them – people with very special abilities, enthusiasm and commitment. And all the signs are that more and more of them will be needed in years to come.

At the moment, more than 400,000 people work within the leisure sector, which in terms of the number of people employed ranks it higher than many of Britain's traditional industries such as chemicals and agriculture. So, although the prospects for making a career from playing sport are as uncertain as ever, they are much more favourable when it comes to leisure as a whole. Whether teaching or coaching sport, organising it for the average person or running a business in the wider leisure spectrum, there's no doubt that its continued expansion makes it a very appealing and exciting area to be involved in.

Part 1

Chapter 1
Professional Sport

Introduction

Many people's working day runs from 9am to 5pm, with an hour off for lunch. With no pressure on them to perform to a high standard all the time, most workers have good days and bad days and, if they are feeling under the weather or fancy a break, they can take sick leave or a week's holiday. Maybe once a year they will be assessed by their manager in a one-to-one interview and their future discussed in a formal way.

Imagine having your work displayed before 30,000–40,000 people and – if it isn't to their satisfaction – having them let you know this in very rough language indeed. Or having to work at a time when you would prefer to be at home or out with friends. Or being blamed for a mistake which could cost your employer thousands of pounds. This is the life of a professional sports player. Your ultimate employer – the general public – is like no other 'boss' because you have very little chance to offer an explanation – and there are newspapers always willing to interpret and misinterpret what you have to say.

There is simply no place to hide in professional sport. It can be an extremely cruel job: one day you are the star, the next you are the fool who made an error and lost your team the vital match. Furthermore, there are no pleas of unfair dismissal or recourse to Employment Protection Acts – you are, quite plainly, judged by your performance. And if that performance starts to decline, you can very easily be replaced. Unless you have made plans for such an eventuality, you may find yourself on the scrap-heap and completely without prospects.

Constant Pressures

Even when you are not actually playing a match or in a competition, your level of dedication must not drop. There is always the fear of someone better coming along to take your place, and resting on your laurels can mean having them swept away from under you.

This means that fitness and alertness – both mental and physical – are vital qualities. You may have all the natural ability in the world, but if someone else is fitter and keener (sportspeople often describe it as 'hungrier') than you, then your chances of succeeding are slim.

Although all this sounds very negative, it is essential that anyone thinking of entering professional sport has no illusions about it. The world of sport is a ruthless and unsentimental place – and while we remember the great names of the past, think how many more we have totally forgotten. Finance and Fate are the governors of sport and its pupils are taken on in a strictly temporary way.

If you become a professional soccer player, for example, you must fit your entire career into the years between about 17 and 32. It is not like joining the Civil Service, where you work until you are 60 and then receive a gold watch and an index-linked pension. Your career can be very short, and when you have left the playing arena for the last time, you have the rest of your life to think about and manage.

Great Rewards

Having said that, it's obvious that *someone* has to succeed in sport, someone has to play football for England or win the motor racing Grand Prix. There is no reason at all why that someone should not be you. As a small boy, Steve Backley will no doubt have dreamed of becoming famous through sport, and as he grew into his teens, discovered that he was able to throw the javelin great distances. Likewise with Tessa Sanderson or any other people who have reached the top; they might have been laughed at by their friends when they wanted to train rather than go to the youth club or the disco, but you can be sure that no one laughs at them now. You can also be sure that the Tessa Sandersons and Steve Backleys of the future are out there with their dreams at this very minute, unknown as yet but destined for fame in the future.

Motivating them will be the prospect of the immense rewards which success in sport can bring, in terms of both fame and fortune. For, as in most high-risk professions, the financial returns are potentially enormous. If you can stretch your career out to ten years or more, taking care to invest what you earn sensibly, then your gamble on entering this precarious world may pay off. You may pocket enough money to last for the rest of your life, or at least a great part of it. Also, if you are lucky, your reputation may open other doors – perhaps in newspaper writing or on TV, or in business, where your success is an inspiration to others.

So, although the pitfalls are many and the competition stiff, there is no reason why you should not be the superstar of tomorrow. However, you have to be determined and committed right from the start.

What, then, are the first things to consider for any young person who wants to enter professional sport?

Getting Noticed

To break into full-time sport, you have to be seen in action by the right people. Some young players are lucky. They represent a school team whose coach or teacher has good contacts with local sports officials – that is, the people who select the district or county representative teams, be it in football, athletics, swimming or whatever. Being picked for your home town or county is the first way of attracting attention from potential employers: as in any profession, word soon gets round about promising newcomers, and if you repeatedly play well, you will find selectors and talent scouts coming from further afield to watch you.

But what happens if your school team coach is not interested in your playing at a higher level or does not know the people to ask, or maybe does not think you are good enough? It is often the case that some schools, perhaps because they lack a good sporting reputation, never have their pupils selected for representative sides, whereas other schools seem to supply half the county team.

Your first step, if you think that your talent is going unnoticed, is to ask your coach to get in touch with the selectors of your local representative sides; there are usually three levels at which you can play, the lowest being for your town's schools side, then the district or borough, and finally the county.

To find out who picks these sides – if your teacher or coach does not know – you should contact the secretary of the regional branch of your sport's governing body.

The Governing Bodies of Sport

These are the organisations which actually run your sport. Every sport has its own governing body and there are some 200 in Britain; you will find most of them listed in Chapter 10 (for example, the Football Association, the National Cricket Association, or the Badminton Association of England). Every governing body has regional offices.

This is how you can find out who selects the local representative sides:

1. Telephone your *national* governing body during office hours (weekdays 9am to 5pm). Ask for the name, address and telephone number of your regional secretary. As an alternative you could write to the governing body, but always enclose a stamped, addressed envelope.
2. Phone your *regional* secretary and ask for the name and address of the person (or persons) who selects the town, district and county sides. For this and future calls you may have to telephone in the evening or at a weekend, as regional officers are almost all part-time voluntary workers and will be out at their full-time jobs during the day.
3. Once you have the name and address of the selector(s), ask your coach or parents to invite him or her down to watch an event in which you will be participating. If possible, give a choice of dates.

Going it Alone

It may be that your coach does not think that you will ever make the grade, or your parents are concerned that sport may interfere with your schoolwork. If you are determined to succeed, you may have to write to the selectors yourself.

Do so as neatly and politely as possible, stating briefly your

achievements (competitions won, medals awarded, etc) and giving dates
and venues for some of your future games. Do not boast or invent
achievements but, on the other hand, do not be too modest. A typical
letter might read as follows:

Dear Mr/Ms/Mrs X,
My name is ———————————————— , I am ———— years old, and I represent
———————————————————— school in ———————————————————— sport.

I am writing to invite you to come and watch one of our matches, and to find
out whether I might be of a good enough standard to represent ———— town/
district/county.

I enclose a list of my forthcoming matches, and would be very pleased if you
could accept my invitation.

Your sincerely

————————————————————

List your achievements, including teams represented, your own performance, and any honours or trophies gained. Then list your forthcoming
fixtures:

> 31 May versus Anytown School, 11.30am at Thistown School, High
> Road, Thistown.
> 5 June versus Othertown School, 11.30am at Othertown School, Lower
> Road, Othertown.

Joining a Club

One of the best ways of attracting attention to your playing ability is to
join a local club which plays your particular sport. Many clubs have
junior or colts sections which will help you to fulfil your potential by
offering coaching and matches against other clubs. Often it is the
performances in club matches which attract attention, especially if
reports start to appear in local newspapers. If your school does not run
teams, then joining a club is easily the best way for you to develop as a
player and to draw attention to your achievements.

To find a suitable club, either:

1. ask the teacher in charge of your sport at school to recommend a
   good club, or
2. find one yourself – you can ask at your local public library, or contact
   the regional office of your sport's governing body, or enquire from
   your regional Sports Council office (the addresses are listed in
   Chapter 11).

Once you have a list of clubs in your area, then you can find out which of
them have players regularly selected for district or county teams. It

would be in your interest to join a club which already has strong links with the selectors. To find out this information, you could ring the secretary of each club and ask him or her. Bear in mind, though, that most clubs want to attract good young players, so don't believe every word that is said! Another way would be to contact the sports editor of your local newspaper; he or she will probably know which clubs are best in any area.

If you are lucky, and keep on trying, you may find that one day a selector will come to watch you play. Of course, this will not guarantee you a place in a representative team; you will have to play to the very best of your ability, and probably on more than one occasion. But if you do manage to make it into your district side, then you have taken the first step on the long, hard road to becoming a professional. Now, let's look at the requirements of the various sports which are played professionally in this country.

Football

Whenever the phrase 'professional sport' is mentioned, it's football that we usually think of. As well as offering the greatest rewards in both money and fame to those who make it, it also gives the greatest number of opportunities.

However, it is also the sport in which the competition is toughest. There are, after all, only 93 clubs in the Football League, each employing an average of 20–24 full-time professionals. Football is also regarded as our 'national game', and it is played by close on two million people on a regular basis. Almost every one of those players will, like you, be dreaming of playing professionally one day and that means that for every place at a league club, there are some 1000 keen and able would-be applicants.

But before getting depressed by the sheer weight of numbers, it has to be remembered that *someone* has to fill each of those places and, providing you're willing to put in the hard work, there's no reason why it shouldn't be you.

Case Study

Kerry Dixon, 31, was a striker with Chelsea before transferring to Southampton. He played 116 games for Reading and scored 51 goals, then moved to Chelsea where he scored more than 120 goals in 250 games.

From the age of 11 I had been visiting Luton Town for training and coaching sessions. My ambition was to play for my home town team, but even though I ended one season as leading scorer for the youth team, the club didn't keep me on as an apprentice. My dad advised me to get a job and play in my spare time, so I joined Chesham United in the Isthmian League and after leaving school took up an apprenticeship with a local firm as a toolmaker.

I then had a trial with Tottenham Hotspur and although I again scored plenty of goals and played a couple of games for the reserves, I wasn't kept on at the club as they had too many strikers to accommodate me. Dad was adamant that I should persevere with my engineering apprenticeship, but the thought that I was just not going to be good enough to earn a full-time living as a professional made me dreadfully depressed.

Then the manager of Chesham moved to Dunstable Town, and I went there too. In my first and only season I finished as top goalscorer in the entire Southern Premier League with 52 goals, and I heard that league clubs were looking at me. I met Reading, who were then in the Third Division, but was determined to resist the temptation to sign full-time as I was about to enter the final year of my apprenticeship and knew the decision would be vital to my entire life and career. Reading agreed to a two-year contract which would allow me to play as a part-time pro and finish my apprenticeship; but as soon as I had done this, I knew the time had come to qualify as a fully skilled footballer.

(From *Kerry – The Autobiography*, published by Macdonald/Queen Anne Press.)

Starting Out

There are three major steps which you must take on the road to playing first-team football for a professional club. The earlier you start, the better your chance of success. Most boys who go on to play in the Football League will have completed step one by the time they are 14.

Step One

You must impress a club sufficiently for them to want to sign you on. As we have said before, this will probably be because you have been spotted playing for your school or county team. The club will then approach you and, through their local 'scout' or talent spotter, ask you to sign Associated Schoolboy forms.

This means that you will go to training sessions at the club, usually two or three evenings a week after school. The agreement you make with the club is rarely for more than a year, but it means that during that time you cannot sign forms or play for another club.

It's important to think carefully before committing yourself to a club, for there could be better offers just around the corner if you wait for a couple of weeks. Also, do not sign any forms before you have talked the matter over with your parents, and they have met a representative from the club. You must also get permission from your school head.

Step Two

Signing on as an Associated Schoolboy, while it might sound exciting to be linked with a professional club, is not really a serious commitment on the club's behalf. They will sign many schoolboys in this way, hoping that a percentage of those taken on at age 13 or 14 will go on to play for the first team. The moment of truth comes at the age of 16, for the club now has to decide whether to sign you as a full-time trainee, on a two-year Youth Training Scheme contract. If they do, then you will have to leave school, and maybe leave home as well if the club is a long way away. In their place will come life on the full-time playing staff, although it will be far from glamorous!

As well as practising and playing, you will have to carry out a range of daytime chores at the club such as cleaning and checking kit, pumping up the balls and sweeping out the dressing rooms. The pay is not huge, starting at £29.50 per week for the first year and rising to £35 per week, with a travel and/or lodging allowance and any 'win bonuses' the club may award.

The club will also insist that you carry on with your studies, as the worst thing possible is to be discarded by a club with no qualifications or experience at all. You may take day-release courses, study for GCSEs and A levels, or learn a practical skill. It is important that you take these studies seriously, for a footballer's career is short anyway and injury or loss of form can always strike to make it even shorter.

Step Three
Now comes the real crunch. At the age of 18 you will either be taken on full-time, or asked to leave. Bearing in mind the fact that most clubs have no more than 25 or so full-time professionals, you can see that only the very best make it. But if you have done well enough to be taken on, you will probably be given a two-year contract and your wages will be no lower than £75 per week.

If you are lucky, and have impressed the coaches and manager at the club, you may be in the first team within months, playing in front of big crowds and the TV cameras – and attracting the attention of the media. If so, then your 'earning power' will quickly increase. You will earn bonus payments for winning matches, and can rapidly achieve the salary of a First Division player – about £1600 per week – not to mention extra money from endorsing products, appearing as a celebrity guest, and opening shops and supermarkets. All these kinds of thing are part of the daily life – and income generation – of a very top player. If your progress is steady rather than spectacular, you may spend a couple of years playing in the reserves before getting a regular run in the first team.

For those who are not successful, however, it's back to where they started – watching from the terraces and maybe trying to make the grade through semi-professional football.

Football Association School of Excellence
For most boys, simply being signed as an Associate Schoolboy is their way into the game, and they must take their chance with dozens of other hopefuls. There are a few, though, whose talent shines out even at the age of 14 or 15 and these players are given the chance to develop their skills with the very best of coaches and facilities at the Football Association School of Excellence at Lilleshall National Sports Centre in Shropshire. These boys are, in a sense, being given a 'fast track' to the top yet they are signed to clubs in the normal way, and combine their football at the School with a normal education at schools near to the Centre.

Set up in the mid-1980s, some of the School's graduates are starting to make their name in the professional game. Hung Da, for example, was a Vietnamese 'boat boy' yet he has a sparkling future with his club, Tottenham Hotspur. England youth international Steve Walters is 17 and playing in Crewe Alexandra's first team in the Third Division – along with three other graduates from the School.

Things to Remember

- You must always talk to your parents before signing any forms. And if they want further advice, they can consult the Professional Footballers' Association, 2 Oxford Court, Bishopsgate, Lower Moseley Street, Manchester M2 3WQ (tel: 061-236 0575).

- Don't be seduced by the glamour of it all and forget that a career in football is, probably more than any other sport, a precarious business. School and GCSEs may seem boring in comparison, but if you are one of those who don't quite make the grade, you will not regret keeping up your academic work.

- When choosing a club, do not be swayed by the big names. Although it might seem thrilling to be part of the set-up at a top First Division side, such clubs have a higher wastage rate of young players than others, and your chances of making the first team are correspondingly reduced. Such clubs can always buy a player to get them out of a mess instead of risking an unknown teenager. It is interesting to note that of the cream of young players at the FA School, many choose to sign for smaller clubs. Steve Walters at Crewe is just one example: he has been able to enjoy success in first team football that would probably be denied him were he signed to a First Division club.

Alternative Routes to Success

Rejection by a league club may be a devastating blow at the time, but it does not necessarily mean the end of all your hopes. Having got so far with the professional game, you should be able to find a place with one of the clubs that play in the numerous semi-professional leagues.

All these players are part-time footballers who do a normal job during the day and then play at weekends and in the evenings - for which they are paid. They will also train a couple of evenings a week.

Although the pay is nowhere near as much as would be earned in the Football League (sometimes it is as little as £50 a week) the standard of football is quite high. Indeed, the success of some semi-pro sides in the FA Cup is proof of this. Many players find that they are quite happy to continue with their daytime careers and earn extra money from the sport they love, but a few are signed by Football League clubs from the ranks of the semi-pros - as, indeed, was Kerry Dixon.

Case Study

Greg Berry, 20, is a professional with Leyton Orient.

> When I was at school I had trials with West Ham, but nothing came of them and so I played all my youth football purely for recreation. Eventually, I joined East Thurrock FC, who play in the Essex Senior League. In my first season I started to play well and I was told that a couple of professional clubs were watching me. At this time, though, I'd left school and had started a job in a bank, and playing professionally didn't really cross my mind: it was just a hobby. I actually thought I was too old to make the grade!
>
> However, the manager of Leyton Orient asked me to play in a youth game for the club, and I was lucky enough to score a goal. The manager then signed me

up on a contract, and I've played a couple of games in the first team when senior players were injured.

Because I wasn't ever an apprentice I missed out on the kind of life where you have to do jobs around the club. My days revolve around training and matches: if I'm playing for the reserves in an evening game, I'll get up about 11 am, potter about the house or take the dog for a walk, and generally relax until I leave at 4–5pm.

Now that I have made the grade as a player, I want to progress as quickly as possible. It's my ambition to play First Division football, but at the moment I'm happy to take things exactly as they come.

Cricket

In contrast to football, there are only 17 possible employers in the world of cricket. That is the number of professional county clubs, and in total they employ about 350 cricketers. Each player is employed to play for just one season at a time, except in the cases of the very top stars, and that season runs only from April to September. For the other six months, technically you will be 'unemployed' and so it is important to realise that, especially in the early stages of your career, you will need 'other strings to your bow' to tide you over the winter months.

Getting Noticed

Most young players are noticed by their counties through recommendation, either by a schoolteacher or club coach. They will put forward their best players for trials, at age groups from under-11 through to under-19. The very best may be selected for their county schools XI, which will play a number of games throughout the summer. In this way, their names will have been noted, and their performances will be watched carefully.

Boys in the older age groups, and very occasionally those in the younger ones, may be invited to go on and play for the county 2nd XI. Although this sounds like playing in the reserve team at a professional football club, in fact it is not like that at all. A great number of players will make the 2nd XI in any one year, many of them hoping, like you, to become a full-time 1st XI player. However, the gap between the 1st and 2nd XIs is very great, probably wider than in any other sport. Most counties use the side as a means to discover whether young players have what it takes to reach the top, and only a handful of county 2nd XI players will be full-time pros on a contract with the club. The rest will, like you, be playing part-time, perhaps in school holidays.

Nevertheless, success in 2nd XI matches is the best way to get yourself taken on to a county's full-time staff. Even if you do not make any appearances in the first team, the experience you gain will stand you in good stead: you will be playing with older pros, some of whom might have been Test Match stars in their day, and with the occasional 1st XI regular taking a chance to recover form or recuperate from injury who is taking a step down to 'look after the youngsters'.

Whether you then go on to establish a place in the full county squad depends on more than just your playing ability. County cricket is not a wealthy sport, even though there is plenty of money to be had from the major cup competitions and the Test Matches. Remember that, unlike football, cricket is played for about six days in every seven during the season, and crowds at county matches are not large. This means that being given a contract may depend on how financially secure the club is at any one time. Bigger counties like Middlesex and Essex have more young players on their books than others, but there is no guarantee that these players will ever make 1st XI regulars.

The County Life

For most professional county players, there is precious little fame and fortune to be had from the game. It is the Test Match players who reap both glory and rewards, with a fee of £1700 per game plus £50 for every ten Tests played, while the average pros do the rounds of the county circuit playing in front of small but appreciative audiences. Furthermore, the pay is not great: at age 19, a player will earn at least £4,250 per season, rising to £5,400 at 20. Being 'capped', which is the sign that your county values your services and wishes to recognise that fact, brings a further increase in salary to a minimum of £9,250.

Players rarely travel in luxury coaches or stay in the top hotels, unlike players of some other sports. They often have to drive their own cars to away matches, stay in modest accommodation and provide their own kit. However, many players are 'sponsored', so that a car and their playing equipment will be provided by companies in return for a few guest appearances at functions.

Many of these sponsors now help to find employment for players during the close season, rather than leaving them to sign on the dole. They may use you as a sales rep, where your reputation as a sportsplayer might help to win contracts, or in public relations and marketing. Some players even work on local radio stations commentating on football and rugby. However, there are always a few who are unlucky, and so gaining qualifications at school is essential.

Hard Work

As in all sports, you need to maintain your fitness, your skills and your enthusiasm to retain a first team place. After all, cricket can be a very demanding profession, as you will be playing six days a week solidly for six months, with overnight travel between games as well.

However, although it is a demanding sport, cricket does have the major advantage that you can play it at the top level for longer than most other sports. Batsmen and spin bowlers, for example, often last until they are aged about 40, while fast bowlers – if they are lucky with injuries – may keep going until about 35.

After retiring, many cricketers go into coaching. This you can do until old age, for there is much less running around needed! It is worthwhile trying to gain some coaching qualifications while you are still a young player, since you may be able to supplement your summer earnings by coaching during the winter in an indoor school – indeed, many counties encourage their players to do so.

Points to Consider

- If you are offered a full-time contract with a county, think carefully before deciding. Cricket is a game in which you generally improve as you mature through your twenties, and it may not be in your best interests to take the first offer that comes along. If you are a good player, rest assured that you will not be forgotten.
- It is worth keeping up your academic studies and even going on to higher education before deciding whether to become a full-time pro. At college you might consider training as a PE teacher, and playing for your county 2nd XI during the summer vacation. The danger is that if you opt to become a professional at 18 or 19, lack of development or a bad injury may put you out of the game by the time you are 21. If you wait that extra couple of years, you will have a sound academic background and qualifications should things not work out; also, you might find it easier to command a place in the first team!

Golf

A recent report by the governing body of golf showed that if the demand for the sport continues at its present rate, literally hundreds of new courses will need to be built. If these courses are constructed, then obviously it's good news for people who want to play golf. But it also helps those people wanting a career in sport – for golf offers the chance to achieve this without necessarily being one of the very top players in the country.

Unlike football or cricket, golf is a game where success or failure depends on you alone. Only you control the way in which you play the game; there are no team mates to let you down or get you out of a mess, no opponent whose bad tackle could end your career. This means that the degree of luck needed for success in a team sport is far less pronounced.

Fortunately, just about every club attached to one of these planned new courses will want to employ a resident professional. The more courses, the more clubs, and the more professionals! Known as 'the pro', this person gives lessons to club members and runs the club shop where equipment and clothing is sold.

As golf is a sport where the peak of physical fitness is not the most important asset, many resident pros are experienced players, perhaps up to the age of 40. However, most pros require assistance, both in the shop and with coaching out on the fairway, and it is through this that you may gain your first foothold in the game.

Becoming an Assistant

The first important requirement is that you must be a good player – certainly with a handicap in a low single figure. Second, you must be aware that the work of an assistant pro is neither easy nor glamorous. You will serve in the club shop, help members with their equipment purchases, repair broken clubs, and do all the paperwork and book-keeping associated with running a small business. The pay can be very low – the Professional Golfers' Association stipulates a minimum wage of just £51.50 per week.

If you wish to coach members as well, you will have to find the time to keep up your own level of performance. Indeed, even to be considered for this you will need a handicap of 4 or less. Better golfers will quite naturally object if they are being helped with their game by someone whose handicap is higher than their own! Therefore, your first challenge is to get your handicap down to the required level and obtain a handicap card from a recognised club. To do this, you will need to join a club and ask to be tested – a procedure which involves playing a number of rounds.

There are quite regular vacancies for assistant pro jobs, and these are often advertised in the sport's specialist magazines, which you will find in any good newsagent.

Prospects

If you apply for an assistant pro's job and are accepted, you will be given a contract by the resident pro. It is to him that you will be contracted, not to the golf club. Before you sign it, however, do seek the advice of someone else, preferably your parents or guardian. Since the pay of an assistant is so low that you will in all probability still need to live at home, it is wise to ensure that the people who will be keeping you know exactly what it is that you're taking on!

If you decide to go ahead, you will first have to pay an initial registration fee of £58.75 to the Professional Golfers' Association, together with an annual fee which will be £82.25 as a trainee. To become a fully qualified pro, you must first work as an assistant for six months. After that, you are eligible to join the PGA's training scheme. This includes on-the-job training over at least three years, and an annual residential course, culminating in a final examination. If you pass, you can then apply to the PGA for election as a full member.

Competitions

Many pros are quite happy to stay in their shops, coach, and play for their club in local matches. Doing just this, they will be able to make a decent living until they are well into middle age. But for some, the lure of the major golf tournaments is an attractive one.

The first step on the road to teeing off with Sevvy Ballesteros is to compete in tournaments in your local area. If you do well in these, then you can apply to the PGA for a 'player's ticket'. However, you must have a handicap of less than 2 in order to do so. This entitles you to enter one of the pre-qualifying competitions in which a small number of the best players will be lucky and receive their 'card' – which gives them entry to the European golf circuit.

Perhaps 50 or so of the top prospects will be fortunate in this way. But of these, only a tiny percentage will go on to take part in the leading tournaments. That's because these have very large qualifying rounds, from which only a few 'unknowns' will get through. It's important, therefore, not to aim too high too soon in golf: if you are determined to become a tournament player you will need to be confident that you can make a success of it, for the earning power of players who fail to make the first round cut is not particularly high.

Further Information
Leaflets on taking up golf as a career can be obtained from: the Professional Golfers' Association, Apollo House, The Belfry, Sutton Coldfield, West Midlands B76 9PT (tel: 0675 470333).

Points to Remember
- The moment that you accept an assistant's job, you can no longer be classed as an amateur and take part in amateur tournaments. Is this definitely what you want?
- Pay for an assistant is so low that you will most probably have to live at home. Are your parents able and willing to support you? If you think of taking a job a long way from home, how are you going to live?

Case Study
Andrew Hanwell, 28, is a self-employed, PGA-qualified golf coach at the Picketts Lock golf course in north London.

> During the winter months, I get in at about 8 am and work in the shop until midday. I then have a couple of hours' break into which I will need to fit any practice of my own, and from about 3pm until as late as 9.30pm I will be giving lessons on the course or the driving range. There are in fact four coaches at the centre and we operate shifts between the shop and coaching. In the summer months the shop alone is open from 7am until 7.30pm, so it's easy to see why we need so much cover.
>
> I see myself as a teaching professional first and foremost, and a tournament player second. Enjoyable though competitions are, it can be hard to find the time for really dedicated practice. Also, I would not like to have to rely on tournament earnings to pay the mortgage!
>
> What I find most satisfying about coaching is seeing novice players get better and better through my own efforts. The hours can be long and there is little time to rest, but for someone who loves the sport, the rewards outweigh the disadvantages.

Horse Racing

Several women have become jockeys in recent years, but one class of person that does not have equal opportunities in this sport is – big people.

At the age of 16, you must still be a mere slip of a lad or lass: under seven stones if you are a boy, under eight stones if a girl. Any bigger, and the poor horse will expend most of its energy simply carrying you along, never mind generating enough speed to win the race.

But if you are light enough and have a genuine love of horses, then you can take the first step to becoming a jockey by applying direct to a horse trainer to be taken on as an apprentice. Alternatively, you can write to the Horserace Betting Levy Board at 52 Grosvenor Gardens, London SW1W 0AU (tel: 071-333 0043) for details of their apprentice course at Goodwood. If you are selected and pass through it, the Board will help to find you a trainer to work for. There is an annual publication which lists trainers, called *Horses in Training*.

An Apprentice Career

Once you are apprenticed to a trainer or a stable, you will eat, drink and sleep horses. Not only will you learn how to look after them and care for their general well-being, but you will learn about the techniques and tactics of racing. Your whole life will be based around the stables, where you will be responsible for exercising and grooming the horses every day of the year, from dawn until dusk. The pay can be very low and is often little more than pocket money after you have paid for board and lodging, but if you are lucky enough to start getting rides at meetings, you can boost your income according to your success.

An apprenticeship ends when you have ridden 75 winners, or have reached the age of 23. However, if you have not ridden enough winners by the time you reach this age, it is unlikely that you would be kept on. This can cause real problems, for while in other sports it's possible to find time to continue with studying, the day-to-day life of a horse-racing apprentice makes this very difficult. There is, then, the danger of being left in your early twenties with few qualifications and no direct career prospects.

Starting Off

Try writing to local trainers to ask if they have any vacancies for apprentices. You will find their names and addresses in the Yellow Pages or on advertisements in the horse and racing press. State your age, weight and experience with horses. The fact that you like the animals will be expected as basic; it will help if you can demonstrate working involvement with them, perhaps at a riding school or stables. Enclosing a recent school report may help if it states that you are bright, eager and willing to learn.

Alternatively, you can write direct to the Apprentice Training School at Goodwood Racecourse, Chichester, Sussex (tel: 0243 527824). The School runs regular seven-week courses for both boys and girls.

Rugby League

In contrast to rugby union, which is entirely amateur, it is possible to earn money by playing the League code of the oval ball game. Although it is still most popular in the north of England, Fulham RLFC have established a sound base for the sport in London, and it seems likely that interest in the sport will continue in the future.

By far the most difficult way to enter the sport is to play rugby union at the highest level. Some union players are adaptable enough to succeed at both, and a number of leading union players have been enticed to League clubs with the promise of attractive salaries and perks. However, if you are not playing at least top-class club rugby union, then the way into the sport will have to be by the more traditional method of playing for a local club and hoping that you are 'spotted', much as in football.

Turning Pro

If you do well with a local club, then talent scouts may invite you to turn pro and play for their club. You will be offered a signing-on fee and a contract for one season. There are, however, very few players able to make a living just from the game. The vast majority have day jobs as well, coming to the club for training on maybe two evenings a week and playing once or twice - in a way similar to semi-professional soccer players. Therefore it is important to have a day job which gives you the time to devote to your sport: self-employment is one option; having a sympathetic employer is another. In fact, many players are employed by their own clubs as barmen, groundsmen, or assistants with marketing and fund-raising.

Pay and Conditions

Jonathan Davies, perhaps the most famous recruit from amateur rugby union, earns sufficient money to live from the game and his various product endorsements. However, there is no minimum wage and many players will only be paid expenses plus a match fee - together with a bonus for winning! Contracts last for one season only and, at the end of June each year, clubs have to publish a list of those players they are keeping on for the following season and those they are letting go.

Tennis

Every summer, Wimbledon Fortnight becomes the focus of British attention. Sadly, however, it's very rare that any of that attention is focused on home-grown tennis players, for our success in the sport has been very limited in recent years. In other countries, better training facilities and support for players have produced more champions than we have, subsisting as we do on lots of 'social' tennis in the local park and not much interest in the more serious levels of the game.

In an attempt to improve this situation, the Sports Council and the Lawn Tennis Association set up the Indoor Tennis Initiative, designed to have more covered tennis centres built and thus offer improved training facilities for those players wishing to try to reach the top. At the moment, though, no more than about 80 players - more men than women - in Britain are able to make any sort of a living from playing tennis.

Getting Started

We often hear how champions from abroad were picking up their first tennis rackets at an age when we were only just past our dummies, and indeed the first step in a tennis career does need to be taken early - perhaps at the age of seven or eight. Many schools and sports centres offer a version of the game called 'short tennis', which gives a feel for the game but without the large court, heavy rackets and bouncy balls. In addition to this, enrolment into the junior section of a reputable club is valuable.

Success in local competitions will start to bring people to watch you, and if you impress your local selectors you may be asked to join a county training session. This can lead to regional training courses via the county team which are organised through the Lawn Tennis Association's regional network.

The next step is to join the national training squad for your age group (under-12, under-14 or under-16), and to attend training weekends or summer school at Bisham Abbey National Sports Centre in Buckinghamshire. Here, the Lawn Tennis Association has established its national tennis centre with some of the very best coaches. Those selected to attend can continue with their academic work for half the day and play tennis the other half. The training is very intense because standards in other countries are so high that great dedication is needed if British players are ever going to compete on an equal footing.

Rewards of Winning

To get anywhere near the national training squad, you must keep on winning the competitions in which you take part, not only the local ones, or even the county and regional ones, but the national ones. For it's a harsh fact that unless you are good enough to play tennis for Britain, you will never be able to make a living from the game – the competition is just too fierce.

As soon as you have reached the age of 16, you are then classed as an adult in the tennis world and are pitched in with people maybe twice your age and with ten times the experience. Only when you have established yourself in the British top 20 or so will you start being invited to play in competitions where the prize money will cover your living and travel expenses.

There is a compensation, however, even if you do not manage to win every professional competition to which you are invited. Even if you fail at the quarter-final stage, say, your achievement is registered on the ATP (Association of Tennis Professionals) ranking list. The better you do, the higher up the list you climb – and the more prestigious the tournaments to which you are asked.

Obviously, how much you earn from the game depends entirely on how good you are – and whether your manager can find you additional income from endorsements, sponsors and the like. But at the start of a career, the bulk of the costs falls on the player – and that usually means his or her parents. While the Lawn Tennis Association makes a contribution towards travel and accommodation costs, it's generally acknowledged that a young tennis player in Britain would find it hard to make the top without strong support – both moral and financial – from parents and family.

Other Sports

There are several other sports from which it is possible to make a living. In some, such as **boxing**, success as an amateur is the way to progress into the paid ranks. In others, like **basketball**, your talents will allow you to progress from a small club into one of the national leagues, from where you may be 'bought' like a footballer by one of the few wholly professional clubs. In a sport like **bowls**, for example, there are now more and more competitions with good prize money for the best players – but few are able to survive entirely by their earnings from the game. And in **real tennis**, many of the top players serve as 'club pros' which covers everything from mending rackets, sweeping the court, giving lessons and handling court bookings, to competing on behalf of the club or as an individual in competitions.

Some more sports which give the chance to make a living to a small number of top players are: badminton, squash, darts, snooker, motor racing, cycling, show-jumping, speedway and table tennis.

Case Study
Colin McMillan, 25, is a professional boxer.

> I became interested in boxing when I was in the fifth form at school, and started to spend my nights alternating between homework and training. I stayed on at school to do my A levels, though, because I wasn't sure that I would ever be able to make a career in boxing.
>
> I had 75 amateur fights and won 60 of them, and reached the ABA final twice and was a member of the British Olympic squad. Then I turned pro on the strength of my amateur career, and so far have won seven out of my eight fights. I hope to challenge for the British featherweight title soon.
>
> However, money is a constant problem. A fighter on the undercard of a bill – even a major one – will not receive much more than about £500. With only about eight fights a year, that means that without sponsorship a boxer needs a day job. I have been a technician with British Telecom for three years, though I want to become a full-time boxer if my agent can find me a sponsor. My employers were helpful to me in my days as an amateur, but they are less so since I turned pro. They obviously think that as I am earning money from boxing, I can fend for myself.
>
> Boxers nowadays are much more sensible in the way that they manage their careers because they realise that only the very best get to where the big money is. Most others simply will not be able to make a living just from their sport.

No-go Areas

Most sport in Britain is still amateur. However, a few sports, although forbidding the earning of money directly from playing them, do provide a springboard to success in later life, because they have made you famous.

Among the many examples of this are the rugby union player Bill Beaumont, who is a TV personality on 'A Question of Sport'; gymnast Suzanne Dando, who has made her name as both a model and a broadcaster; and modern pentathlete Kathy Tayler, now a television presenter.

It's also possible to earn a living from athletics, although in an indirect way. Any money you earn from sponsorship and endorsement is put into a trust fund, from which you can draw your living and competition expenses as you need them. The remainder is kept for the end of your career, when it is shared between you and your sport's governing body. Obviously, not all athletes would earn enough to be financially secure for the rest of their lives but certainly the likes of Steve Ovett, Sebastian Coe and Steve Cram would be in that happy position.

The Sports Aid Foundation

In recognising the problems which amateur sportsmen and women have in simply making ends meet, the Sports Aid Foundation offers small grants to struggling competitors. The Foundation is a voluntary body which raises its money from charity events, national raffles and the like, and although the grants it makes might be small – perhaps just £30 or so a week – they can be a lifeline. If you feel that you deserve a grant to help you reach the top in your sport, and are of international calibre, then contact the Foundation at 16 Upper Woburn Place, London WC1H 0QN (tel: 071-387 9380). The money is granted after an application has been made on your behalf by your sport's governing body.

Chapter 2

PE Teaching

Introduction

Being a school PE teacher is probably about the most secure job there is in sport. No one is going to sack you because the school netball or football team has lost every game in the season! And PE is a foundation subject in the National Curriculum and will therefore continue to provide career opportunities.

But that does not mean that it is an easy job. Not only are you on your feet throughout the school day and often beyond, but you must constantly be on your toes in order to keep things moving and to provide interesting activities for your class. You should have a commitment to working with children and young people, and lots of stamina and patience as the work is demanding.

Nevertheless, despite the physical pressure, PE teaching is a most rewarding career to go into. It keeps you fit, sporting and young, and there can be enormous pride and satisfaction in watching your pupils' talents develop. However, it's not all sport - teachers in secondary schools have to be prepared to teach one other subject, maths or English for example, and in primary schools the whole range of subjects has to be taught.

Qualifications

Teachers in schools must have a degree. The usual route is through a specific university, polytechnic or college course which will result in a Bachelor of Education (BEd) degree, but students can take a different degree course and follow it with a Postgraduate Certificate of Education (PGCE) in Physical Education. The basic requirements for most of these courses are five GCSE passes which must include English and maths, with three passes at A level and, normally, an active interest in sport must be evident.

What College?

There is no shortage of colleges and universities offering degree courses in PE and related subjects (see Chapter 10 for a list of these). Before you start applying, however, you must make an important decision – do you definitely want to be a teacher of physical education?

If the answer is 'yes' then you should choose a three- or four-year course. If the answer is 'not sure' then you should consider doing a three- or four-year BA or BSc, involving PE, but not how to teach it, and decide at the end whether you want to go into teaching; if you do, a further year's study, either at the same or a different college, will give you a teaching qualification.

Case Study

Heather Lowden is a PE teacher at a mixed secondary school in Hertfordshire.

At the age of 14 I was into all kinds of sport, both in and out of school, and though I didn't excel at one particular sport, I was in a couple of school and club teams. I thought sport was great fun, and when I had to think of a career I knew that it had to be in sport, much to the distress of my careers adviser at school who tried to push me into something more 'academic'. But I knew what I wanted, so I got the necessary qualifications and went to Dunfermline College to do a BEd in Physical Education.

At college I got a rude awakening as we had to spend a lot of time in lecture halls, and a lot less time out on the sports field than I had imagined. Looking back, the lectures were vital, even though at the time I thought it would be better to be out practising sport!

I thoroughly enjoyed the stints of teaching practice we did while at college, but after I got my degree I knew I had to have some time off – school, college, school seemed just too claustrophobic. I would advise anyone taking up any kind of teaching to do this – you have to get out into the real world for a breath of fresh air!

After a year, I took up a teaching post in Edinburgh at a mixed secondary school, and from there moved to Switzerland to teach PE for a couple of years. You don't have to stay in this country to teach – there are lots of opportunities abroad for qualified teachers. On my return, I settled in Hertfordshire, where I have taught in a variety of schools. My job involves me in teaching just PE all day every day, though I do have some input into personal and social education classes. My mental attitude is that sport in school is primarily for enjoyment, secondly to learn new skills and very rarely for elitism. I am very conscious of providing for the children a broad, balanced curriculum that they find good fun.

My job is very rewarding and very exhausting. I run clubs at lunch time and after school, and at this school we still play matches at weekends, so free time is scarce. However, I think in the next ten years PE teachers will see their jobs change radically with the introduction of the National Curriculum bringing lots of paper work and bureaucracy, and the introduction of GCSEs in sport and dance making the subject more academic and less physical.

Finding a Job

You should start to look for a job long before you leave college. The number of schools in Britain is falling, in line with a decrease in the number of children, so jobs aren't that easy to come by. However, because so many school-leavers are finding it harder to get jobs, schools are increasingly looking to broaden their curricula beyond standard academic subjects and more towards living skills and under this heading PE plays an increasingly large part. Hence, there is a demand for PE teachers who are interested in sport not just as a means of keeping fit but also as a means of developing character and self-reliance in their pupils.

You can find advertisements for jobs in papers like *The Times Educational Supplement*, the *Guardian*, and all the newsletters and magazines of the various teaching unions. Every college running educational courses will have copies of these in its library.

Secondary or Primary School Teaching?

At primary schools, PE teachers are expected to take a whole range of subjects; at secondary schools they will probably only have to take one other, and will have more time to concentrate on PE. The level of sporting skill among primary-school children is much less developed, maybe causing frustration for the teacher who is keen to promote success. You must decide in which age group and at what skill level you want to work.

Pay

The amount you are paid is laid down according to the geographical location of your school. Teachers in Inner London are paid the most, teachers in Outer London less than those in the city centre but more than those outside the designated area. A teacher in Newcastle will earn about the same as a teacher in Exeter. Nevertheless, a PE teacher in both primary and secondary schools will start on a salary of around £10,000 per year.

How to Apply for a Course

If you want to go to university, the competition for a place will be tough, but the qualification all the more prestigious. You will need to get an application form from the Universities Central Council on Admissions (UCCA), PO Box 28, Cheltenham, Gloucestershire GL50 1HY. You should do this in the autumn of the year before you start the course. The academic year runs from October.

On the application form you will have to list your six choices of university in order of preference (see the UCCA handbook for lists of courses at each university, and ask your careers adviser for prospectuses of those universities). The universities you have listed will offer you a place immediately, or offer you a place conditional on your getting certain A-level results, or ask you in for an interview, or reject your application. Make sure that you consult with both your parents and careers adviser throughout this process.

A similar procedure applies if you would prefer to go to a polytechnic, college or institute of higher education. For polytechnics, your application should be made to the Polytechnics Clearing Admissions System, PO Box 67, Cheltenham, Gloucestershire GL50 3AP. PCAS is in the process of merging with UCCA (1992) since polytechnics now have university status and are currently choosing their new names. Applications should be made direct to colleges and institutes of further education, though they do recruit candidates through both of the above systems, after those systems have rejected applications.

Lists of colleges, polytechnics and universities offering PE teaching qualifications appear in Chapter 10. A guide to the colleges and institutes of higher education is available free from: Administrative Officer (guide and leaflet), SCOP, Edge Hill College of Higher Education, St Helens Road, Ormskirk, Lancashire L39 4QP (tel: 0695 75171).

A Word of Warning

Although it is great fun being a PE teacher in your twenties, thirties and even forties, after that it can become both physically taxing and mentally unrewarding. If you are going into PE, therefore, do not neglect your other subject, or subjects, of a more academic nature. Although they may seem dull alternatives when you are young, they may provide you with a career lifeline when you are older.

Further Information

Advice and information on PE teaching as a career are available from the Physical Education Association, 162 King's Cross Road, London WC1X 9DH (tel: 071-278 9311).

Chapter 3
Coaching

Introduction

Millions of people take part in some sort of sport on a regular basis, resulting in the need for a vast number of coaches in an enormous variety of sports. All participants in every sport require the help and expertise of a coach or instructor to get them started or, if they have talent, to enable them to develop their abilities to the full.

Besides an in-depth knowledge and thorough understanding of your sport, to be a coach the most important quality you need is enthusiasm. You need to care about your performers as human beings to help them to realise their potential. You need to know how the mind and body works and how people respond to exercise and competition. You should be a good communicator. Patience, tact, optimism, perseverance and the ability to inspire confidence are the necessary personal attributes. Good organisational skills help, too. Plus, of course, you must have the capacity to take a back seat – people tend only to be interested in the star player, not the hard-working coach.

If you haven't coached before, you could start by reading the National Coaching Foundation's Introductory Study Packs, available from the NCF, and perhaps attending some of their courses. Contact the NCF at 4 College Close, Beckett Park, Leeds LS6 3QH (tel: 0532 744802). Many coaching jobs are combined with administration and other work, so coaching may only be part of the job.

Work Environment

Coaches work in a wide range of situations – gyms, sports centres, playing fields and outdoor pursuits centres – in almost all weathers. They have to be present at training sessions and competitions, resulting in very long working hours in the season, and they have to work in the off-season preparing training programmes, often when the performer is resting. Coaches tend to work unsociable hours: most sports competitions and matches take place when other people are free to watch or participate, such as evenings and weekends.

Qualifications

Every coach must hold the appropriate qualification from the sport's governing body (governing body addresses appear in Chapter 10). Each sport, through its governing body, has its own award scheme which provides training opportunities for coaches of all levels. Books, videos and training courses can help you on your way, as can watching coaches who already practise.

Full-time Coaching Jobs

Full-time jobs are very scarce. Professional sport is a very competitive business and coaches tend to be judged by success. Sometimes a coach may stay in one job for several years and establish a reputation for getting results. Consequently, talented individuals are keen to work with them and will often seek their guidance. In many instances, these coaches are ex-professional sportsmen and women who have also gained top coaching qualifications from their governing body. Opportunities vary from sport to sport. Professional sports like soccer and cricket have a long tradition of employing professional coaches, but nowadays there are full-time coaching opportunities in ice-skating, horse riding, golf, swimming, squash, tennis and water sports, among others. There are opportunities for full-time coaching jobs with the governing bodies of sport (national coaches), local authorities, outdoor centres, holiday camps, private hotels, leisure centres and large sports clubs.

Case Study

John Derbyshire was a professional sailing coach. He was responsible for the coaching of two British Olympic teams participating in the Seoul Olympic Games in 1988. He now works for the Sports Council as a Sports Development Officer.

I qualified as a sailing instructor when I was 18 by undertaking a number of awards set out by the Royal Yachting Association (RYA). At that time I was also a top-class dinghy racer myself. When I left school, I did a degree in teaching (BEd) and taught at a secondary school for a couple of years. During this time I spent a lot of time sailing, picking up more RYA teaching awards. I decided to further my teaching qualifications by taking a postgraduate course in Physical Education. The following summer I got a job as a sailing instructor at what was then the National Sailing Centre (NSC) in Cowes.

Initially, my position as a racing instructor was on a shared basis between instructing on courses at the NSC and coaching for the governing body, the Royal Yachting Association. My coaching responsibilities were involved mainly with Olympic teams. When the NSC closed in 1987, I was seconded by the Sports Council to the RYA until October 1989. My responsibilities were expanded and included two Olympic classes, coach training and development and a national fitness testing programme, as well as areas of youth and women's sailing.

Following the Olympic trials, I coached our representative on a one-to-one basis. A typical training week generally ran from Monday to Friday, with weekends off unless there were competitions or events. We started early each morning with a couple of hours of physical training on a graded programme, after which we sailed for about four hours, depending on the wind. During the sailing time we weren't just practising skilful moves with the boat, we had to do lots of equipment testing of the mast, sails and hull, to find out which combinations worked best. This was necessary because at the Olympic Games the boats to be used were different from the one our representative qualified in. Practical sailing was followed by a physical warm-down, then a debrief and discussion of the day's events. At this time we meticulously recorded all the data on personal and equipment performance. Two or three evenings a week were spent visiting mast- and sail-makers, or on further coaching.

But my job wasn't all sailing. I was responsible for organising transport, accommodation, food and the shipping of boats whenever we went away to competitions. I was the leader, the organiser and the motivator.

After the Olympics, I continued to coach for a further year, but I felt that it was time to move on. The disadvantages of long, unsocial hours and personal sacrifices had taken their toll. But I realise I was very lucky as vacancies for professional coaches are extremely rare. And it was great fun at the time. I now coach on a pick-and-choose basis, and I'm enjoying the freedom of being able to sail and take part in competitions myself again.

Paid but Part-time Jobs

Most sports have a need for coaches on a part-time basis. These are generally attached to sports centres and private clubs, and are paid according to the number of hours they teach. Although this type of coaching does not carry the security of a full-time job, it may provide enough money to live on. But working part time allows the coach to continue instructing, as well as to hold down a completely different full-time job. Most coaches are in their twenties and thirties, so you will need something to fall back on when you are older, less fit and less enthusiastic about the activity.

Unpaid Jobs

Every sport, without exception, needs unpaid coaches. After all, a large proportion of sport in Britain is played by amateurs in their spare time, at clubs and grounds where everyone – officials and players – does it for fun. Even Steve Ovett's coach, Harry Wilson, who coached him for nearly ten years, was a man who worked for the Engineering Industry Training Board and spent all his free time coaching the young athlete!

In some cases unpaid, dedicated coaching can actually lead to full-time paid work, since a number of the governing bodies do appoint paid coaches or 'technical directors' to run a national team or supervise their sport in one particular part of the country. The men and women they choose will undoubtedly have come from the ranks of loyal, amateur coaches who have already given years of unpaid service to the sport.

Pay

Pay in coaching varies enormously from sport to sport. National governing bodies employ coaches on fixed contracts and for fixed salaries. In professional sport the pay very often depends on how much prize money is earned, how well a particular team or individual is doing, and how popular the sport is for spectators. Coaches are likely to get a basic salary with bonuses for good results.

For those who are self-employed, particularly part-timers, the amount they earn depends on how many people they are coaching, at what level, and on the success of their students. Coaches in this situation generally charge their clients a fixed sum for every hour they instruct.

Self-improvement

One way of speeding up the transition from amateur to professional coach is to take the one-year, full-time course at Heriot Watt University's Moray House Institute of Education. It is called the Diploma in Professional Studies (Sports Coaching) and is open to anyone who has a good practical record in coaching, either on a professional or voluntary basis. Diploma holders have much less trouble in finding paid work, although it can never be entirely guaranteed that a job will be forthcoming, or that it will be in Britain. For more information contact Moray House Institute of Education, Holyrood Campus, Holyrood Road, Edinburgh EH8 8AQ (tel: 031-556 8455).

Outdoor Pursuits Instructors

Outdoor pursuits instructors are more and more in demand these days as the opportunities for enjoyment that exist in the countryside become increasingly popular. Thousands of people use the outdoors for walking, climbing, canoeing, mountaineering, skiing, orienteering and sailing, among other sports, many of them through courses or holidays run by outdoor pursuits centres and activity holiday centres. These centres are usually in an area close to a wide range of natural resources – hills, sea, lakes, rivers and mountains – and instructors must be prepared to work in such areas.

Outdoor pursuits instructors must be proficient in a number of sports, such as those mentioned above, hold the relevant governing body instructor awards, and have lots of practical experience.

Even though job opportunities are growing, most of them are at the basic instructor level and many are seasonal. Even fully qualified staff with loads of experience won't have a clear career path. Competition for the few senior jobs that exist, as full-time instructors at Plas y Brenin and Glenmore Lodge (the National Centres for Mountain Activities) for example, is very severe. Pay is generally very low – often accommodation and pocket money are the rewards for long working hours. It is the quality of life that attracts people to this job.

Case Study

Marcus Bailie is an instructor at Plas y Brenin, the National Centre for Mountain Activities. He was a member of the International Nile Canoe Expedition which made a five-month descent of the River Nile, and has subsequently paddled in Africa, Canada, USA, Mexico, Chile, Nepal and New Zealand, as well as making many trips to Europe.

Canoeing is my first love. I started to canoe at university. Over the next few years I took a number of the British Canoe Union (BCU) instructor awards, and have been a qualified BCU coach since 1983. I have an honours degree in maths and I am a trained and qualified teacher. I have worked in outdoor activity centres since I left university, but only on a full-time basis since I came to Plas y Brenin four years ago. Prior to that, the work was mainly seasonal, and I have spent periods of time teaching maths to A level in secondary schools.

In outdoor pursuits you can't specialise in just one sport. Here at Plas y Brenin we teach skiing, canoeing, orienteering and mountaineering from beginners right up to the highly skilled, as well as instructors of the sports. I have acquired, through my work in outdoor pursuits, a variety of other qualifications, like the Mountain Instructor's Certificate, that enable me to coach in these sports. Teaching outdoor pursuits isn't just about knowing how to instruct - canoeing and climbing are dangerous sports that can't be taught from the river bank or the foot of the mountain - the instructor has to be highly skilled. The students I teach want to have both an exciting and a safe time and they trust me to look after them, so I can't be seen to do anything that looks dangerous or inexperienced in their eyes.

My job isn't all practical teaching. At Plas y Brenin I am expected to help in the administration of the centre, work in the equipment rooms and give lectures to students on a variety of outdoor topics. But in return, I've got the opportunity to develop and practise my own ideas about the theory of teaching outdoor pursuits.

The days at Plas y Brenin are long and I am expected to work both weekdays and weekends, depending on the particular courses I am involved with, but there are lots of advantages to being an outdoor pursuits instructor. I have the opportunity to practise the sports that I enjoy, I have access to the necessary equipment, I live on the doorstep of some of the best canoeing and climbing country in Britain, and I constantly mix with people who enjoy the same sports as I do.

Chapter 4

Recreation Management

Introduction

As recently as 1970, there was really no such profession as 'recreation management'. There were barely 20 sports centres in this country; now there are more than 1500. Each of these needs trained staff to manage and run it, so that in just two decades a whole new profession has been developed. What is more, there is little doubt that it will keep on growing, as people have more free time and are aware of the benefits of leading a healthy life.

A recreation manager is someone who, quite simply, organises the provision of our recreation – not so much checking that the badminton nets are at the right height, but ensuring that the day-to-day working of the sports venues within his or her orbit is as efficient and effective as it can be.

Case Study

Sue Biggar, 38, is general manager of the Jubilee Hall Sports Centre in Covent Garden, London.

> Jubilee Hall is located right in the centre of London, and is open seven days a week, from 7am to 10pm. We have a full-time management staff of just seven, plus part-time instructors and supervisors, and the facilities we are responsible for include a multi-sports hall, a large weights room, dance studios and a café.
>
> I work an average of about 50 hours a week, and my responsibilities range very widely. For example, today I began by writing to the local council to negotiate a new building, then I helped out on reception, then I did the accounts and banking, then I wrote a brochure, and at about 5pm I will have to work on reception again as this is our busiest time of the day.
>
> I have been here for 11 years, and my background is actually in the arts, not sport – though I have always enjoyed playing games and exercising. What I most enjoy is the fact that we operate in a collective sort of way, so that we get together with the various heads of sections on a regular basis to discuss the way the centre is run. And even though the hours are long and unsocial – sometimes it feels like having a service job, where you are at the beck and call of others – there is a buzz, an excitement, about working in a place such as this. I like the fact that I'm involved in something which is actually good for you, and there is a very creative atmosphere about the place.

As Sue Biggar's 'typical day' shows, working in recreation management need not be solely about sport! In fact, her work demands leadership, good organisation, a head for figures and the ability to put together sentences for a brochure. What about actually being good at sport? It certainly helps, but it is far from essential – provided that you are deeply interested in and committed to sport. What this means is that recreation management offers a chance to work in sport and leisure to those young people who love sport, but need not be brilliant at playing it.

Getting Started

There are various points at which you can enter the leisure profession:

- From school, with GCSE qualifications at age 16/17.
- From school, with A levels at age 18/19.
- From a college, with vocational qualifications at 18/20.
- From higher education, with a relevant HND/degree at 20/23.
- From higher education, with a postgraduate qualification at 22+.

Entry from School

At the age of 16 or 17, there are two jobs which you can go straight into. The first is a parks worker (see Chapter 5), and the second is a swimming pool attendant.

In the latter case, you will stand a much better chance of getting a job if you hold a BTEC (Business and Technician Education Council) Diploma or a CGLI (City and Guilds of London Institute) Certificate in Recreation and Leisure Studies. These can be acquired by taking courses on either a part-time or full-time basis, and even on a Youth Training Scheme. Both these courses will include practical work placements and the chance to take sports coaching awards. You will find a list of colleges offering these courses in Chapter 10. Competition for jobs at the foot of the recreation management ladder is very intense, and you will need to show that you are keen, willing to learn and committed to the work.

As a pool attendant, you will have to carry out a number of basic tasks, but they are vital ones. Most importantly, you will watch over the swimmers and ensure that the pool is orderly and that no swimmer is in trouble. To do this properly, you will need to have the Amateur Swimming Association's Basic Certificate in Life Saving; your employer (the local council) may help you to gain this, but it would greatly help your chances were you to pass it before applying for a job. Either your local swimming pool or the ASA (see address list in Chapter 10) will be able to tell you where you can take this easily achieved qualification. A swimming pool attendant will earn about £6,000–£7,000 a year.

If you are entering the profession with only GCSE qualifications, you will need to gain some more practical qualifications to help you climb the ladder. ASA coaching badges are a help if you enjoy working in pools and would like to move up to the next step, which is that of senior baths supervisor. You can also attend part-time courses, either during the day or in the evening, to gain the NEBSM (National Examination Board for Supervisory Management) Certificate in Recreation Management or

Supervisory Management. Your employer may help pay for you to take these courses. An NEBSM certificate will help you to move over to work as a supervisor in a 'dry' sports hall, too. Colleges offering NEBSM courses are listed in Chapter 10. If you have stayed on at school to take your A levels you may be able to enter the industry direct, but there are not many trainee posts. Indeed, you may find that you have to 'step back' to basic level posts for a while, simply to gain experience. However, your better academic qualifications will help you with your continuing on-the-job training, perhaps on a course leading to a BTEC Certificate in Management Studies or BTEC Continuing Education Certificate.

Case Study
Alison Webb, 24, is a recreation officer at the Marshall Street Baths in central London.

Although I went into higher education after leaving school, I didn't complete my degree as I was more interested in getting out into the 'real world' and starting a job. I spent a summer working for an outdoor activities company, then took a casual job as a lifeguard at a pool near my home in Bedford. I'd already gained the general Bronze Medallion for swimming, but in this job I was able to take the Medallion for poolwork.

The work at Bedford was mainly lifeguarding and a bit of instruction, whereas my job at Marshall Street has given me more responsibility – I am in charge of staffing and organising cover if people are off sick. This is useful, as I would eventually like to manage a multi-sports complex with more than just a pool.

At the moment, though, I still have to do my shifts of pool duty like the other lifeguards. One week I will work from 7am to 2pm, then the next it'll be 10.30am to 6.30pm, and then 2.30pm to 10.30pm. I also have to work one Saturday in three – the pool is closed on Sundays as it's in the middle of London and not many people would want to use it then, so at least we all get one regular day off.

Any kind of work involving a swimming pool is hard and tiring because you have to concentrate all the time and can't relax or turn away for one second. There are also busy times when you have to be extra vigilant, such as early in the morning, during the lunch hour and from about 5.30 to 7pm.

Even though the hours are long, it's good to work in a fun, sporty environment, and I do feel that I'm being given the chance to learn and develop my skills.

Vocational Qualifications

The BTEC National Diploma in Leisure Studies is a course from which many students move into the leisure industry after finishing college. Its strong vocational element will certainly be an advantage in finding a job, but it is important to stress that it will not guarantee one. Leisure is no different from most other professions – it seeks not the academically brightest of candidates, but the most 'rounded' people – those who can combine academic skills with those of a personal nature, such as a positive attitude to work, self-motivation, discipline, good organisation and a pleasant character.

Senior Baths Supervisor

If you are promoted to this position, your work will have more responsibility attached to it. You may be responsible for supervising other junior attendants and handling the day's takings. You may even have to deputise for the pool manager in his or her absence. At this point, you will have to decide whether to stay in swimming pools and specialise in the subject, or to broaden your general recreation experience.

If you stay with baths, you can progress to baths manager or maybe begin to specialise in the technical aspects. Pools are complex pieces of engineering and their heating, ventilation and filtration systems, for example, need management by people who understand all their workings. To do this, you will need to gain further qualifications, usually through part-time courses. These are run by the Institute of Baths and Recreation Management (IBRM), Giffard House, 36–38 Sherrard Street, Melton Mowbray, Leicestershire LE13 1XJ (tel: 0664 65531).

If this appeals to you, then you will have made a wise career move. The growth in popularity of lagoons and 'leisure pools' seems sure to continue over the next couple of decades, and the Sports Council is committed to building and refurbishing a number of traditional pools in the coming years.

Sports Centre

If you decide to move away from the swimming pool, you may be able to do so by applying for a job as a supervisor in a sports centre, perhaps in a 'wet/dry' centre (which has both a pool and a sports hall).

A sports hall supervisor is responsible for what goes on inside the building, and the work can be very varied. It might include coaching (so coaching certificates are useful), and will definitely include looking after equipment, helping with enquiries from users, and supervising the players and bathers during opening hours.

Although the job is lively and 'sporty', it can be tiring as the hours are long and unsocial. Sports centres are at their busiest when other people have finished their day's work, so the hours from 6pm to 11pm can be the hardest of the day – which means that working in a sports centre is not for anyone seeking a comfortable 9 to 5 job. Pay usually starts at about £6,000–£7,000 a year, and you will have a chance to continue with your education. Some employers will ask you to take an NEBSM course during your employment (see Chapter 10 for a full list of such courses).

Moving up to Management

The jobs listed above are of a manual, rather than managerial, nature. However, to make the move up to the next level – assistant manager of a sports centre – it is necessary to obtain an academic qualification. The most usual method is to take a DMS (Diploma of Management Studies), which includes courses on accountancy, industrial relations, sociology, marketing and media skills. Usually, you can only take a DMS after you have been working for five years or have taken a degree. This is because your DMS must be fitted in around your daytime job, perhaps involving one day a week at college, and your employer may pay for your course fees (about £450 in year one, £760 in year two). He or she will need to be sure that you are committed to your career before doing so, and length of service is a good indicator of this.

Assistant Manager

At this level, work starts to have far greater responsibility. You may find yourself in charge of the sports centre for certain periods, especially in the evenings, and your job will be a mixture of day-to-day organisation and longer-term management. For example, you may have to deal with an unhappy customer, a theft in the changing rooms, a mislaid key, a shortage of squash balls and a blocked pipe in the ladies' loos – all within ten minutes. When you have sorted out all those problems, you might be involved with some of the centre's financial matters, such as buying new equipment and maintaining stock control.

Again, the hours can be long and unsocial, and you will always need to present a smiling face to your centre's users. At this level, however, your performance will be watched and good progress will open the doors to higher management.

Deputy Manager

The 'number two' will need to be capable of running the centre without blinking an eyelid if the manager is called away or goes on holiday. The deputy will also have particular areas of responsibility and be in complete charge of, say, catering or publicity. This person is often in charge of selecting staff and interviewing for jobs.

Manager

At the top of the ladder is the manager, who is in charge of the centre and responsible for everyone who sets foot inside it. However, as Sue Biggar's typical day showed earlier, the manager's job can be much more about administration than sport. The manager has to plan the way in which the centre is run, bring in new ideas and see that they are carried out effectively, anticipate which type of people the centre is appealing to, and ensure that people with disadvantages – the unemployed, the physically handicapped, for example – are able to use the centre as they would wish. The manager also has to speak on behalf of the centre to the local council, who will usually be subsidising its running (very few sports centres make a profit), and if it is not developing as the council would like, answer some awkward questions. The manager needs to be a diplomat as well as all those other things!

The manager of a medium-sized sports centre would expect to earn about £14,000–15,000 outside London, with managers of very large centres commanding salaries well over £20,000. Good performance is often rewarded with a bonus scheme, and the very best managers will receive a 'package' of benefits worth about £30,000. As leisure becomes more important in our society, so its top practitioners can earn very handsomely.

Taking a Degree

It can take many years to reach the management level in leisure if you have to work your way up from the bottom, but a degree will help you to 'leapfrog' the initial stages.

There are numerous colleges now offering BA or BSc degrees in recreation management. Each course is different – some may have special components in accountancy, business management, sociology, sports science, etc – so to find out exactly what each entails, you will need to write to the various colleges for a prospectus. This will outline exactly what the course comprises during its three or four years and state the qualifications needed for admission.

The Importance of a Degree

There is no doubt that as leisure management becomes more important, and the expertise of those within it becomes greater, there will be fewer posts for people without degrees, especially in more senior positions. Provided you have the academic qualifications (at least five GCSE passes and two A levels), it is far wiser to aim for a degree than to try to work your way up.

Remember, though, that college is a costly business. You should be able to obtain a grant for your tuition fees, but you will also need money for food and accommodation. At the moment this can be provided by your local education authority, but the introduction of a 'student loan' scheme may make you responsible ultimately for paying back your grant. You will probably need at least £2400 per year to live on.

Once you have read through the various prospectuses, decide which colleges appeal to you most. You will then have to apply through UCCA (the Universities Central Council on Admissions) or PCAS (the Polytechnics Clearing Admissions System) which have set procedures for applications to higher education establishments. A merger of these organisations is in train. If your application is well received by the colleges you have chosen, you will be asked along for an interview on the strength of which they will reject you, accept you unconditionally or, more likely, accept you on the basis that you achieve certain A-level grades.

A Non-sport First Degree

If you are not yet sure that you want to follow a career in recreation management, but are definitely interested in going on to higher education, it may be best to take a first degree in the subject which you find most interesting. This could be English, applied mathematics, law, or whatever. Once you have graduated, you can take a DMS or postgraduate course in recreation management to give you the background for that particular career.

Case Study
Rachel Fowler, 28, took a first degree in General Arts, specialising in English, before moving into sport.

> At university, sport was very well organised and it was easy to get involved in it, but at that time, I had never really thought of it as a career. It was the PE Director who suggested that I should try to do so because it seemed to him that it was the area in which I had most interest. So I applied to Loughborough University and completed an MSc in recreation management – basically a management degree but with an orientation towards recreation.
>
> After graduating, I was appointed Sports Development Officer on one of the Sports Council's Action Sport schemes. I progressed to become Community Recreation Officer in Southend, and am now Leisure Development Officer with Gosport Borough Council. In this job, I am responsible for all outdoor recreation that isn't facility-based. I find the work very rewarding and it offers constant challenges and responsibility. Each day is different, and I'm usually out of the office and meeting people which means that I get a lot of job satisfaction from seeing the results of schemes that I've helped to set up.
>
> Looking back on it, I'm pleased that I took a non-sport first degree because I feel that studying recreation only would have been limiting. Also, my English is now extremely useful in report and tender writing and for general good communications.

The Local Authority Recreation Department

Rachel Fowler's job with Gosport Borough Council brings us to one of the most fertile areas for recreation management graduates: the council leisure department. This is a rapidly changing area as many departments are undergoing a process known as competitive tendering, ie the running of sports centres can be put out to private companies if they can do the job as well as the council but at a cheaper price. This process is bringing more and more people into leisure departments in order to manage the change.

A recently advertised job specifies exactly what councils look for in their staff:

> 'You should be educated to degree level, preferably in a recreation-related discipline, and have experience within a leisure facility. A positive interest in sport and leisure is essential, together with a clear analytical approach to problem-solving, good communication skills, and the ability to work to deadlines.'

As with management positions in a leisure centre, you can see that there is a lot more to the work that just helping people to play sport!

Recreation departments have well-defined ladders of progression, and from the basic job of leisure officer, you can progress to a senior leisure officer post and even to director of leisure. This job is highly responsible and has a large 'political' element. It involves managing a budget of many millions of pounds, and being responsible for the entire provision of leisure activities in the area. Not surprisingly, it is very demanding and pressurised, but salaries reflect this – in a large metropolitan council the director of leisure may earn more than £40,000 per year, together with a range of benefits.

If none of the above appeal to you there are several other ways in which a dedicated young person can make a career in recreation management.

Sports Leader

This is one job in sport for which you do not need any academic or professional qualifications at all. What this work does require, however, is the ability to inspire and motivate – and keep control of – other people, whether they are excited teenagers or more sedate older men and women. It is also important to have skills in a wide range of sports, a characteristic which helps enormously when you are trying to get other people interested in them.

Life as a sports leader is physically and mentally demanding, with long working hours often spent in far from glamorous inner-city areas where much of your task is simply to keep otherwise unoccupied young people out of trouble. Yet the rewards are there, too, particularly when a project you have been working on comes to fruition and the success is largely down to you.

The Central Council of Physical Recreation (CCPR) runs a non-professional Sports Leaders Award Scheme, which is intended for voluntary helpers of sports clubs and youth groups. It is a structured training scheme supported by the governing bodies of sport and although it has no direct job opportunities, some sports leaders have been able to find work in leisure centres and many others have been encouraged to take further coaching and proficiency awards to equip them for a career in sport. For details, write to the CCPR, Francis House, Francis Street, London SW1P 1DE (tel: 071-828 3163).

Many professional football clubs have set up community sports programmes in recent years, drawing the club and the local community closer through coaching sessions for youngsters, and work with people with disabilities and the unemployed. Steve Williams, for example, is Football in the Community Supervisor at Tranmere Rovers FC. He looks after 12 trainees whose job it is to establish coaching schemes, run them and organise other community events such as bingo sessions for pensioners.

Job advertisements for sports leaders can be found in the national press, and in recreation management magazines (such as *Leisure Opportunities*, *The Leisure Manager* and *Leisure Management*).

The Sports Council

The Sports Council is a government-funded organisation set up to promote the development of sport. England, Scotland, Wales and Northern Ireland all have their own Sports Councils, though the last three are on a smaller scale. The Council headquarters are in London, and in England it employs more than 500 people in nine regional offices. Jobs for the Sports Council include processing grant applications from governing bodies, sports clubs and local authorities; advising on the technical design and management of sports buildings; working in 'sports development' – helping clubs, governing bodies and associations both to encourage more people to play sport and to get the very best of them to play even better.

Case Study

David Henwood, 26, works for the Sports Council's Facilities Unit:

> I did a BA joint honours degree in Sports Studies and English at West London Institute of Higher Education. I'd always enjoyed sport, but even though the Institute is a traditional PE teacher training college, I knew that I didn't want to be a teacher. As the three years progressed I became interested in sports administration, while the fact that my course was half-devoted to English was also useful, as it meant I had 'another string to my bow'.
>
> After graduating, I applied to Loughborough University and took an MSc in Physical Education and Sports Science. I also learned about the structures of sport, and it was actually through my research thesis on this subject that I gained a job with the Sports Council. I interviewed a senior member of staff about the role of the Council, and she asked if I had seen the advertisement for a post in its Central Policy Unit. One week later, she was interviewing me for the job!
>
> After working in that unit, I was promoted to Executive Officer (Recreation Management) in the Facilities Unit. Here, I am at the hub of the Sports Council's task in the planning, development and management of sports facilities throughout the country. What I find exciting about this is that I feel right at the very centre of what is going on in sport.

The Sports Council also operates five national centres – Bisham Abbey, Lilleshall, Holme Pierrepont (National Water Sports Centre), Plas y Brenin (National Mountain Activities Centre) and Crystal Palace. The staff here have roles more akin to sports centre managers.

Sports Council job advertisements appear in the national press and in local papers. To find out more about the work of the Council, contact either its London headquarters or one of the regional offices (see Chapter 11).

The Commercial Sector

Perhaps the biggest growth in the world of leisure in recent years has come in the commercial sector. As sport and recreation have turned into big business, more and more private gymnasiums, health and fitness clubs and sports centres have been developed. These cater mainly for the more 'exclusive' end of the market, and as such have different require-ments of their staff. Whereas local authorities are often tied to rules stipulating what qualifications their employees must have, commercial firms are not bound by these. They may often take on people with no formal recreation management qualification as such, purely on the strength of their personality. Also, career structures are less rigid and so the most talented can progress very quickly, far more rapidly than would be the case in a large public sector organisation.

However, most private sector clubs are run in extremely professional and streamlined ways, and opportunities for people without qualifications are diminishing quickly.

The kinds of managerial progression possible in the private sector are actually similar to those in the public sector, with a scale moving up through 'section managers' to the ultimate club or gym manager. However, the main difference in the work is that in private enterprise, money and profitability are always the bottom line and business skills are extremely important. A facility manager must constantly be thinking of ways to attract new members and provide a better service for current ones so that they use the premises more often, thus bringing in more revenue.

Often, management experience in only slightly related areas, such as hotels, is useful in this sector of leisure. But, just as the pressures are greater, so are the rewards. Commercial sector salaries usually run at some 30 per cent higher than those in the public sector, and there is a constant flow of skilled people moving from public to private in search of the greater earning potential.

Perhaps the most likely way of getting a foot on the private sector ladder is as a coach or instructor. To do so, you will need both experience and qualifications, plus that vital extra ingredient – a strong, understanding, sympathetic and approachable personality.

Case Study

Dan Collins, 27, is Gym Manager at Cannons Club in London's Covent Garden.

I originally wanted to be a professional footballer, and was on the books at Watford. But as I also did well at school and stayed on to do A levels, I wasn't as 'tunnel-visioned' as some of the apprentices and thought I was better off combining a career with good class, semi-professional football.

I went to college and took a BSc in Sports Science, but while I was there I suffered a badly broken leg, which effectively ended my footballing hopes. While at college I qualified as an FA coach, and after leaving I worked in the USA coaching at sports camps. On my return I also qualified as a masseur, thinking that this might be a way into the sports world. It wasn't, but one of the clubs to which I had written, Cannons, offered me the chance to take on odd jobs in return for free membership. Within two weeks I was using my sports science background in helping out in the gym, and soon this turned into full-time work. When Cannons planned a second club in London, I was lucky enough to be asked to become Gym Manager.

My typical day might start at 9am, when I will begin cleaning and maintaining the equipment, planning the daily timetable for fitness assessments, and allocating staff tasks. I might get the chance for a workout of my own some time during the morning. At lunchtime and in the evening I work as a gym instructor, although I have overall responsibility for the way that the place functions. So as well as helping customers with their individual programmes, checking exercise techniques and making sure the equipment is used correctly, I have to ensure that my staff are doing what they should and that our clients are getting all they wish from the club.

I usually leave at about 8.30pm. Though there is a shift system for the instructors, there isn't one for me. I have to work whatever hours I feel are necessary, and these are long ones. However, I don't think you come into this profession expecting anything less.

There is no central register of private fitness and sports clubs, but your regional Sports Council office will have details of those in your area.

The Sports Trade

There are now several major exhibitions of sports clothing and equipment every year, proof indeed that the 'sports business' is a fast expanding one. Companies both large and small are constantly bringing out new and exciting products and ranges of clothing, and this is an area of the sports world that offers increasing career prospects.

One way of entering it is to work for a manufacturer. Companies need people who understand the needs of sports players to help sell their products to retailers, and working as a rep will bring you close to games in which you have an interest. Such jobs are often advertised in local papers, and you will need to be bright, articulate and well-presented. A fondness for sport is also important as you may have to talk in technical terms about some of the equipment you are promoting. Many of the largest companies also have technical departments which research into new products, and for this kind of work you may need to have a scientific background.

A second way is to work for a sports shop in your local high street. These tend to be small, private businesses, often run by one person, so it may be best to call round in person and ask if there are any vacancies for serving assistants. For this work you will need to be friendly and at ease with customers, able to talk knowledgeably about the equipment and clothing on sale, and confident when dealing with customers' requests.

If you are interested in working in the sports trade, more information is available from the Federation of Sports Goods Distributors, 20 Costells Edge, Scaynes Hill, Haywards Heath, West Sussex RH17 7PY (tel: 0444 831410).

Further Information

An excellent source of information on all matters to do with recreation management is the Sports Council Information Centre, 16 Upper Woburn Place, London WC1H 0QP (tel: 071-388 1277) which is open from 10am to 4pm for phone calls and personal visits.

Chapter 5
Groundsmanship

Introduction

It's a sad fact that most sportspeople only remember the pitches they play on if something is wrong with them. The cricket wicket where the ball popped or shot along the ground, the rugby pitch where the grass was cut too short, the tennis court where bare patches caused the ball to deviate: these are the kinds of thing that players remember long after the actual result has been forgotten.

As for the elegantly manicured bowls green, the expertly marked football pitch or the perfectly true croquet lawn - who gives them a second thought? We tend to take it for granted that our sports grounds should be without fault and don't really stop to think about the hard work that's required to make them so.

If it is the outdoor life that you are after, then groundsmanship is a career well worth considering. It is a highly skilled job, needing a lot of practical experience; it is also a vital job, for without playable pitches the 'Game off' signs have to be put up, spoiling everyone's sporting plans. Indeed, in many cases the ability of the groundsman is what stands between a game being cancelled or going ahead. The groundsman has to be a weather forecaster, an expert on turf, soil, fertiliser and all the other ingredients of a pitch, a capable handyman - and a dedicated worker. For all that, great personal satisfaction will be gained from seeing sport played without problems on a pitch that he or she has prepared. And at the very top levels, a groundsman at a Test Match cricket ground is one of the most important people for the captains to talk to in order to discover how the pitch is going to 'play'.

Getting Started

The usual way to start work in groundsmanship is to begin at the bottom, as a parks worker. Most of these jobs are with the local council and are usually advertised in the local newspaper or at the Jobcentre. However, a lot of the posts are dependent on your having some experience, which you can gain by doing temporary work in the summer as a relief worker. Again, these posts are often advertised in the local paper during the spring. If you wish to check, then contact your town hall or council office.

The tasks performed by a general parks worker are first of a manual nature – shifting leaves, cutting hedges and grass, and so on. As you progress, you will start to learn not just how to mow a lawn effectively but also about the make-up and characteristics of soil and grass. In fact, many local authorities now have a well-developed training scheme, established by the Local Government Training Board, under which you can qualify as a 'craftsman groundsman' by doing either a one-year, full-time training course or receiving on-the-job training at your park. The full-time courses are organised by the City and Guilds of London Institute.

Becoming a Craftsman Groundsman

Exactly how long it will take you to become a craftsman groundsman depends on both your commitment and ability, and the willingness of your employers to allow you to take the various training courses. Five years is about the minimum time, but once you have the qualification your skills will be in great demand: there is a general shortage of skilled and experienced groundsmen and women, mainly because of the lack of glamour associated with the work. Remember, however, that your ability will earn you the respect and admiration of the players.

Another way to become a qualified groundsman is to work in the private sector and then study in your spare time – or, if your employers are willing, to go on a day-release course – to gain the National Practical Certificate, which is administered by the professional groundsmen's organisation, the Institute of Groundsmanship. After that follows the National Technical Certificate, which requires more detailed scientific knowledge of soil, fertilisers and grass, then the Intermediate Diploma, which involves a grasp of general sports ground maintenance and management. Finally, after you have had at least six years' experience, you can take the National Diploma. This is the highest qualification, and it is likely that by the time you take it you will have worked your way up into a supervisory position, probably at the Parks Department or within the private company for which you work. Although many groundsmen choose not to move into this more administrative type of work, it is an option if the outdoor life becomes too demanding.

Women in Groundsmanship

There is no reason at all why groundsmanship should be a male preserve. Indeed, many women have achieved success in the profession and gone on to supervisory and managerial positions within it.

Greenkeeping

One of the most highly regarded areas for a groundsman to move into is that of golf greenkeeping. There are very few sports where the quality of the grass is so crucial to the sport, and the skills of the very best greenkeepers are much sought after.

As golf becomes an increasingly popular sport, so there is a general shortage of greenkeepers qualified to look after courses. The British and International Golf Greenkeepers Association has been set up to help change this. They will advise on entering greenkeeping as a profession – from grass-cutting level to golf course management – and they have established the Master Greenkeeper Certificate for those attaining the relevant qualifications and experience within the profession. Thirteen approved colleges offer the National Vocational Qualification (NVQ) Level 1 in Golf Greenkeeping, and the Higher National Diploma (HND) in Golf Course Management is offered at two colleges. For further information contact the British and International Golf Greenkeepers Association at Old Walk Manor Hotel, Halme, York YO6 2NS (tel: 03473 581). They will provide a list of the approved colleges and courses.

Pay

The basic pay of a local authority parks worker will be about £150 per week, though overtime can boost this figure. In the private sector, wage rates vary both above and below this amount. In the specialist area of greenkeeping, the British and International Golf Greenkeepers Association has specified minimum wages: these range from about £150 per week for an assistant or older apprentice to more than £18,000 per year for the head greenkeeper of a major 36-hole course, and to over £35,000 for the head greenkeeper of a championship course

Case Study

Groundsmen and women have much more to think about than simply cutting the grass and marking out the cricket pitches correctly. At Queens University in Belfast, the head groundsman, David Herron, has 77 acres of grass play areas to manage. The university has 21 registered teams and, in addition, there are more than 40 society teams which organise their own competitions. With so many players wanting to use the facilities, it can be a real headache trying to accommodate all the fixtures. Some pitches for certain sports have to cater for four or more games a week, and in the months from October to March there is always the risk of their turning into complete mud baths.

As well as tractor-mowing the grounds, David Herron and his team have to carry out re-seeding programmes every spring and operate to a tight schedule for general maintenance – in addition to the everyday tasks of rolling, cutting, marking out and repairing the pitches and wickets for a huge number of different sports.

Chapter 6
Sports Medicine

Introduction

Sports medicine has made great advances over the last ten years in this country. As active participation in sport has been recognised as a means of improving the health of the nation, greater emphasis has been given to both individual health improvement and injury cure and prevention. Thus, there are a greater number of people involved in the physical care of both sportsmen and women. Sports injuries cut across the whole range of medical specifications – from mending broken bones to dealing with sprained and torn ligaments. There are three main types of sports medicine practitioner – doctor, physiotherapist and osteopath. The doctor is involved in actually 'mending' the injury and the physiotherapist and osteopath in aiding and speeding the patient to full recovery.

Doctor

There are no full-time doctors employed by the National Health Service who deal exclusively with sports injuries, though there are a number who work in this area on a part-time basis. However, several private sports injury clinics have been set up around the country and they devote themselves solely to the study and care of sports injuries.

How to Start

Prior to specialising in sport, you must first qualify as a doctor, or general practitioner (GP) as they are sometimes known. This is a lengthy and demanding process. It takes seven years – six at medical school and one as a house doctor in a large hospital – and requires high academic achievement. Initial qualifications to enter medical college are five GCSEs and three A levels, one of which must be biology and all of which must be of a very high grade. Medical schools are tied to universities, and applications to study medicine should be made through UCCA, as for any other university degree course. Any queries should be directed to the British Medical Association, BMA House, Tavistock Square, London WC1H 9JP (tel: 071-387 4499). You might also like to read *Careers in Medicine, Dentistry and Mental Health* (Kogan Page).

There are a number of courses in sports medicine available to doctors after they have qualified. The British Association of Sport and Medicine runs one-week courses in sports medicine. They can be contacted through the BASM Education Officer, London Sports Medicine Institute, c/o Medical College of St Bartholomew's Hospital, Charterhouse Square, London EC1M 6BQ (tel: 071-253 3244). The London Sports Medicine Institute runs three-year, part-time courses for doctors and can be contacted through the General Secretary at the above address. There is a one-year, full-time diploma course in sports medicine for doctors at the London Hospital. Details are available from the Course Administrator, The Diploma Course in Sports Medicine, G I Building, 26 Ashfield Street, London E1 2AJ (tel: 071-247 9183), and the Edinburgh Post-Graduate Board for Medicine run one-week courses in sports medicine. They can be contacted at Moray House Institute of Education, Cramond Campus, Cramond Road North, Edinburgh EH4 6JD (tel: 031-312 6001).

Physiotherapist

As with becoming a doctor, you have to first become a qualified physiotherapist and then specialise in sports injuries. Physiotherapists are specialists who do much more than simply massage or treat broken bones. They are expected to treat people of all ages with a wide range of illnesses and conditions, from breathing problems to relaxation classes, as well as educate the public to help prevent injury. Once qualified, it is largely up to physiotherapists to gain experience in whichever area interests them, and it is at this point that they can make sport their specialisation though it is very rare that they will be able to do this full time in the UK. There are opportunities in the small number of sports injury clinics scattered around the country, and in some professional sports like football and athletics, but a great number work mainly in another area of physiotherapy and voluntarily or privately for sportsmen, sportswomen and clubs in their own time.

Case Study

Vivian Grisogono is a private physiotherapist specialising in sports injuries, and an active sportswoman. She travelled as an unpaid physio to the British team at the Winter Olympics in Moscow in 1980 as well as to many other international events.

I first became interested in becoming a physiotherapist when I injured my back playing tennis. There was no one who could help me regain my fitness until I met a physio who got me back on the tennis court.

After I had qualified and gained a few years' experience working as a physio, I moved into the area which interested me most and, in time, I set up the first full-time sports injuries clinic within a national sports centre – at Crystal Palace. I had to learn how to treat injuries as I went along. The techniques involve only basic therapeutics, but you have to know a lot about sport to apply therapy to injured sportspeople. You have to fit your treatments into the context of their sporting aims and be extremely patient – because your patients aren't!

There is not a lot of scope for earning a full-time living through treating sports injuries except by practising as a private physiotherapist. If you are known in sporting circles, you tend to attract people by recommendation – our professional code of conduct forbids us to advertise our services. In the past this has led to a situation where unqualified practitioners are often better known than genuine chartered physiotherapists offering an ethical service. However, this has changed since the initiation of the two-year diploma course as certificate holders are recognisable as experts in ethical and efficient sports injury treatment.

How to Start

Both men and women work as physiotherapists. In addition to the academic qualifications, you will need to be a good communicator, tolerant, patient and caring. Physiotherapists are also required to be physically fit. It is a demanding job that often requires the strenuous manipulation of a patient's limbs.

Just over half of all physiotherapy students take a degree course at either university or polytechnic; the remainder take the graduate diploma course in schools of physiotherapy which are usually attached to general hospitals. The entry requirements are much like any other degree or diploma course, and in general students need a minimum of five GCSEs and two A levels. Some schools require specific subjects to be studied, and as competition for places is high, it is unusual to be accepted with only minimum grades.

Physiotherapy courses usually last three years, though there are four-year honours courses in London and Belfast, and successful students will receive a BSc in Physiotherapy or a Graduate Diploma in Physiotherapy. It is at this stage that students can specialise in sport.

For further information about becoming a physiotherapist, the universities and colleges that provide degree courses and the schools of physiotherapy, contact the Chartered Society of Physiotherapy, 14 Bedford Row, London WC1R 4ED (tel: 071-242 1941) and ask for a copy of their booklet, 'Physiotherapy: A Career in a Caring Profession'. For information on the diploma in sports physiotherapy contact the Royal Liverpool Hospital College, School of Physiotherapy, Prescot Street, Liverpool L7 8XN (tel: 051-709 0141).

Osteopath

There has been a significant growth of interest over the past few years in the techniques and results of osteopathy – a method of treatment for injuries which, although it does not conflict with conventional medicine and is effective in complementing it, is still not recognised by the National Health Service. Osteopathy involves the manipulation of joints and bones to promote recovery after injury. The results are often swifter than traditional methods of treatment and because it is only available through private clinics, treatment is available as soon as, and as often as, it is needed.

How to Start

Like physiotherapists, osteopaths have to deal in a very direct way with patients, and so the ability to communicate easily and effectively is essential. You will also have to be understanding and sympathetic as many of the people you will be dealing with will be in great pain and probably very frightened initially. All students who qualify as osteopaths are able to find jobs in the profession, and as there are many centres in Britain which still do not have the services of a registered osteopath, the choice of location is wide. Each year some graduates find jobs abroad. There are no jobs for osteopaths in the National Health Service.

If you want to train to become a registered osteopath you need to qualify at a recognised institution such as the British School of Osteopathy. They run a full-time, four-year course from which you will gain a BSc in Osteopathy. The general entrance requirements are five GCSE passes, with two of them at A level and in science subjects, preferably chemistry, biology or physics.

For further information contact the British School of Osteopathy, 1–4 Suffolk Street, London SW1Y 4HG (tel: 071-930 9254).

Chapter 7
The Sports Business World

Introduction

There's no doubt that sport is big business. You only have to watch the television to see the number of major events that attract not only lots of spectators, but also advertisers and sponsors. In fact, sport in Britain would find it difficult to survive were it not for the money fed into it by businesses, advertisers and sponsors.

There is also an increasing amount of money to be made by the players themselves: not only from the prize money they receive by winning tournaments, but by business deals in which they endorse products. That is, they literally 'sell their names' to be put on items as diverse as breakfast cereals and cricket bats.

Such players need professional advisers to help them through the various problems which the business world can throw up. These advisers are also the kind of people who arrange the events themselves, and the skills which they need are very diverse.

Accountants and lawyers in particular can move into sports management; however, it is essential to have first gained significant experience in traditional accountancy and the legal profession. Sport may be an exciting business, but it is business all the same.

Getting Started

First, you must obtain qualifications and experience in business, perhaps as an accountant or solicitor or through working in marketing and public relations. While doing your daily work in these professions, it may be that some of your clients will come from the sports world and, if you are able to, it would be useful to try to handle their particular concerns.

Barry Hearn, the snooker and boxing promoter and man behind the Matchroom snooker business, qualified as an accountant before he moved into sport. He was able to apply his specialist knowledge to a sport that was then very badly organised and promoted, and in ten years turned it into a multi-million-pound industry.

Barry Hearn also started his career as a manager by acting for a young, unknown player called Steve Davis. Looking after a sportsman or woman in your spare time is another way of entering the sports business world; it may be that an up-and-coming young player is seeking advice and help in his or her early years, and would be glad of any extra income you might be able to find, after you have taken your cut!

There are opportunities for working in the business of sport in both the public and private sectors. Each, however, will be looking for enthusiasm and expertise, together with a host of bright ideas.

Case Study
Bob Peach is the Sports Council's Commercial Manager.

An economics degree was followed by a career in the advertising industry before going to the Sports Council. I have also been involved in sport both as a participant and an organiser for numerous years, and my job now gives me the chance to combine professional expertise and personal interest to make a worthwhile and rewarding contribution to the development of sport in the community.

The Sports Council is a government-funded organisation, but it has the ability to generate its own income from sponsorship and endorsement. It is my job to help find companies interested in supporting the activities of the Council, and to put together schemes which operate to the benefit of both. For example, a major bank is currently funding a national project to attract more young people into active participation. I have to ensure that the sponsor gets its 'money's worth' in terms of publicity and media coverage, and that both the sponsor's and sport's interests are properly considered.

It's the kind of work which demands good analytical skills, coping with long-term financial and planning projections and, most importantly, the communications skills to co-ordinate the different views of several organisations. The hours can be long and the pressure sometimes quite intense – so it's essential to have a calm and balanced temperament.

As the development of community life gives more scope for major leisure activities, I feel that opportunities for a career in sports marketing will undoubtedly increase.

However, the business world is one where talent and an understanding of the subject can count for more than academic qualifications.

Case Study
Frank Burke, 23, is Press, Publicity and Promotions Officer with the sports event promoter, Frank Warren.

My background is very ordinary. I didn't go to college, but I did gain an A level in film and photography and have always been interested in creative design and the media world. After school I travelled abroad for a while and on returning found what sounded like an interesting job advertised in an agency: to work as a 'runner' in a leisure company. A runner is a person who starts at the bottom making the tea, but gets the chance to see how a business operates and learn about the various jobs. The company was the one I am still with, and although I had to make the tea as well, I could see that the people there were willing to listen to my ideas about things like poster design. They took up my concept for a bill poster advertising a McEnroe *v* Edberg tennis match, and soon allowed me to have complete control over the creative side of the business: the publicity, media relations and design work.

I realise that I am very young to be in such a responsible job, but Frank Warren started in business when he was young and I think that he respects enthusiasm in young people. Formal qualifications aren't really necessary for the work that I do – enthusiasm and a willingness to start at the bottom and work my way up are more important. But it is hard work, and I'd say that only about 40 per cent of the job is pure pleasure. The rest is a very challenging mix of pressure and commitment.

Chapter 8
Sports Journalism and Photography

Introduction

It is, as everyone knows, a lot easier to be an armchair sports critic than to be out there on the field. However, have you ever thought about making a living out of it? There are numerous jobs in Britain for people who either want to write about, or take photographs of, sport.

Sports Journalism

Writing about your favourite sport, the Olympic Games or even the FA Cup, and getting paid for it may seem like a dream come true, but you can't just walk into a job like this. Consider how many national newspapers there are, each of which probably has only four or five full-time sports reporters. The sum total doesn't add up to many journalists. There are opportunities to travel, to meet top sportsmen and women and to attend world sports events, but only a handful of journalists ever get them. But if you're talented enough, lucky enough and you have solid experience covering the less glamorous areas of sport, you may well find yourself out in Italy covering a World Cup Final. Sadly, few women work as full-time sports journalists for the national press, but the situation is changing. However, there are opportunities to work on the sports desk of local and district newspapers and specialist sports magazines.

Case Study

Louise Taylor works on the Sports Desk of *The Times* as a football, netball and sports politics reporter.

> I did a degree in Law at Durham University, and when I graduated I tried to get a job as a journalist but was unsuccessful. I decided to go abroad for a while and got a job teaching English as a foreign language in Cairo. While I was out there I wrote some freelance articles about the traumas of supporting Sunderland Football Club, which to my amazement were published in the *Observer*. Thanks to this, on my return I was offered a place on a graduate trainee scheme for journalists, run by the Thomson International Organisation. Through this I spent five months on a local paper up in Newcastle, and when I completed the training, was offered a job on the *Middlesbrough Evening Gazette*. I actually hated it there and left after two months, but it turned out to be a lucky move. I have always been a football fanatic, supporting Sunderland, and dreamed that one day I would be paid to write about the sport. On my departure from Middlesbrough, *Match*

magazine, the football weekly for teenagers, offered me the chance to work as a journalist for them on a trial basis. I had, a few months earlier, written to them on spec, and it had paid off! While I was at *Match* I did weekly reports on football matches for the *Observer*, and in July 1987 I decided to leave the magazine and freelance full time as a sports reporter. I worked regularly for both the *Observer* and *Today* newspapers, but in April 1988 I started regular freelance work for *The Times*. I am now based at *The Times* as a 'roving sports reporter', though I am still freelance, covering mainly football, netball and sports politics.

There's a lot of hard work involved in being a journalist – mainly I work from about 10 o'clock in the morning until around 8 o'clock in the evening, and if I'm covering a football match then I have to work evenings and weekends – but I love it.

How to Start

The first point to note is that there is no simple route into sports journalism. Very few people join a national newspaper straight away – most first gain experience on a smaller local newspaper or a magazine. To become a sports journalist, it is advisable to train to become a journalist first and then specialise.

The Local Paper

If you find a job on a local paper you will first become a general reporter, covering all sorts of local events – crimes, fêtes and council meetings, among others. As time goes by you will begin to develop a preference for, and a skill in, certain areas of news, and if you're keen on sport you should let this be known to the editor. There is usually no shortage of sports events to be covered, especially at weekends, and if you do well you may be allowed to start covering sport full time, perhaps as an assistant sports editor.

One advantage of the sports department is that it is often slightly independent of the rest of the paper, and this means that you will also gain valuable experience of the other skills of journalism – page layout, commissioning photographs and writing headlines. This will stand you in good stead if you want to move to a bigger paper where jobs are much sought after and a journalist with layout and subbing skills may be of more use.

Magazines

A harder way of getting into sports journalism is to find a job on a sports magazine. Look on the shelves of any newsagent and you'll see that there is no shortage of them.

To join a sports magazine you will probably have to commit yourself to one particular sport – most sports magazines are aimed at the participants and followers of a particular activity – be it sailing, football, cycling, squash or cricket, or any other sport you care to mention. Unless you are very interested in that sport, you may soon tire of covering nothing else and you can become 'branded' a cycling writer, for example, and find it difficult to find work in another area. Think twice before going straight for a specific sport magazine job.

How to Apply
There are several ways of joining a local paper or magazine.

Direct Application
Find out the addresses of a number of local papers near your home, making sure you have the name of the current editor. Write to each editor explaining that you would like to be a journalist, and would like a job on the paper. List as many interests as you can – the editor will be looking for an all-rounder, not a sports fanatic – and enclose a copy of your Curriculum Vitae (See Chapter 9 for details). Don't worry if he or she answers that there are no vacancies. Write back and offer to send in regular reports on local sports and social events – if these are used it will stand you in good stead when a vacancy does come up.

An NCTJ Course
The National Council for the Training of Journalists (NCTJ) recommends special one-year pre-entry courses for young people wanting to start on a local paper. There are eight of these courses, based at colleges and polytechnics in Darlington, Harlow, Portsmouth, Preston, Sheffield, Cardiff, Edinburgh and Belfast, and they are designed to give students a full grounding in the basics of journalism.

Courses generally run from September to July, and applications should be made a year before the course begins. Applicants considered suitable must first take a written test during the autumn and, if successful, must attend an interview before Easter. Further details can be obtained from the Director, National Council for the Training of Journalists, Carlton House, Hemnall Street, Epping, Essex CM16 4NL (tel: 0378 72395) except for students wishing to take the Edinburgh course (which lasts two years), and the course in Belfast. They should contact Napier University of Edinburgh, Murchiston, Colinton Road, Edinburgh EH10 5DT (tel: 031-444 2266) or the College of Business Studies, Brunswick Street, Belfast BT2 7JX (tel: 0232 245891).

For courses in England and Wales, applicants must have at least two A levels and two GCSE passes, one of which must be in English.

All who pass the examinations at the end of the year generally have very little difficulty in finding newspapers willing to take them on – the college will help in placing them. Once on a paper, the young journalist usually goes on a three-year training apprenticeship known as indentures.

The NCTJ also runs a number of short courses, usually lasting from two days to a week, aimed at both newspaper and magazine journalists who want to undertake advanced training to supplement their skills.

Graduate Entry
While a degree is not essential to get a job in journalism, as with many jobs, entry requirements quoted are a minimum and places will often go to the best qualified applicants.

It is possible to enter journalism at postgraduate level, following a postgraduate diploma in journalism. There are four courses, held at the University of Wales College of Cardiff, South Glamorgan Institute of

Higher Education, Cardiff, City University, London, and University of Central Lancashire. A graduate with a postgraduate diploma in journalism stands a very good chance of landing a job on a newspaper.

Some of the very large publishing organisations also run graduate training schemes. The competition for places on these schemes is very intense and applications involve submitting written work. College and university career advisers will be able to provide more detailed guidance, but if you would like to make your own enquiries contact:

> IPC Magazines, Stamford Street, London SE1 9LS (tel: 071-261 5000). The Thomson Organisation, Bourne House, 34 Beckenham Road, Beckenham, Kent BR3 4TU (tel: 081-650 4866).
> Reed Business Press, Quadrant House, The Quadrant, Sutton, Surrey SM2 5AS (tel: 081-661 3500).

Case Study

Michael Walsh is the Editorial Assistant on *Sport and Leisure* magazine.

> I always wanted to be a sports journalist – at school I was interested in both playing, and reading about, a wide variety of sports, especially football, and I enjoyed writing – so taking a degree in Media Studies at the Polytechnic of Central London seemed a logical step.
>
> The first year was very general: we did a term each of radio, video and print studies, after which we had to specialise in one particular area. I chose print, and spent the next two years developing my journalistic skills, writing about all sorts of things – from the environment to music. I kept up my interest in sports writing throughout my course by helping out in the *When Saturday Comes* office. I didn't get paid for my help, but I reckoned it was good experience and it gave me an idea of how magazines were produced in the real world. It also convinced me that sports writing was what I wanted to do.
>
> When I left college I didn't specifically look for a job on a sports magazine or paper – I wanted to get some experience and would have worked for any publication, but the right job came along at the right time. Working on *Sport and Leisure* isn't all big events and superstars; there are a lot of mundane tasks to be done, but equally there are lots of interesting and exciting things to write about.

Radio and Television

There are very few jobs as sports reporters and presenters on television and most go to journalists who have prior experience of working in the sports press or national newspapers. See *Careers in Television and Radio* (Kogan Page).

Numerous colleges offer courses related to the media, and students whose interests are in radio journalism should make their choice very carefully. Entry into radio journalism is primarily postgraduate and competition is very strong, though those of a good academic standard equivalent to a degree may be considered.

Sports Photography

The basic requirement of any photographer, working in the sports field or elsewhere, is reliability. What's news today isn't news tomorrow. Your reputation as a photographer is based on the pictures you produce. The photograph you see in the morning paper might have been taken the night before in driving rain and freezing conditions. And, unlike any other photographer, the sports photographer has only one split second in which to catch the action – you will not be given a second chance if the picture is underexposed or out of focus. You cannot ask Gary Lineker to score the goal again just because your light meter did not register the first time!

Constant alertness and technical expertise are the two primary requirements of any photographer working for a newspaper, and more especially for the sports pages. Sports picture editors are looking for action – goals, wickets, injuries and fights.

How to Start
There are very few full-time opportunities for those wanting to work as professional sports photographers. The majority of sporting pictures are taken by photographers who are self-employed and sell their pictures to newspapers, magazines, periodicals or picture agencies. It is advisable to train to become a competent photographer and then specialise. Don't be put off by thinking that you need lots of expensive equipment. Initially, your flair for taking an interesting picture will shine through regardless of the price of the camera.

A Photography Course
There are numerous photography courses around, many of them part-time evening courses, those run by local education authorities being the most popular and least expensive. There is one official pre-entry photographic course approved by the National Council for the Training of Journalists: the Press Photography Proficiency Test, held at Stradbroke College in Sheffield. You stand a very good chance of getting a job on a local paper if you reach the required standard on this course. To qualify for acceptance you must have one pass at A level and five GCSEs including one in English. Applicants are also required to take a written test and, if they pass, attend a selection interview.

A Photographic Studio
As an assistant in a photographic studio you can expect to do everything except take photographs – making the tea and answering the telephone will be among your daily duties. But if you stick with it you should be trusted eventually to do simple photographic assignments. This is a very hard beginning for a photographer and the pay is very low. However, you will learn a great deal. If you feel that you would like to start your photography career this way, simply contact all the photographic studios in your area – you will find their addresses in the Yellow Pages. They will normally ask to see some photographs you've taken in the past.

Working Freelance
Freelances are self-employed photographers who take pictures and then try to sell them to a wide range of publications – from newspapers to

textbooks. Most will have attended a photography course and very few will specialise in only one area such as sport. Freelancing is very hard work and requires a great deal of self-discipline, but it can also be very rewarding. If the freelance is well-known he or she may be commissioned by the sports editor of a newspaper to cover a particular event, in which case a day's income from taking pictures is guaranteed.

Case Study
Richard Gardner is a freelance photographer.

> I did a two-year course in Documentary Photography at Newport College of Art and Design as I didn't know what to do and I enjoyed taking pictures. The course was very practical and structured around the principle that photographers have to work for a living after they leave college, relying on their own ability to create a design or image that will sell. Students were encouraged to put a portfolio together to set them on their way.
>
> I have freelanced since I left college basically for whoever is willing to pay me. It's not an easy option – it's hard work. I have to sell pictures by physically knocking on the doors of newspapers, magazines and periodicals and finding out their photographic requirements. There is plenty of work, but only on the assumption that you can produce the photographs that people want and that you have a good business sense.
>
> Photographers need to be prepared to work unsocial hours and to develop their photographs very quickly. I think it's important for photographers to be realistic about their own capabilities. If I have any doubt about whether I can take certain pictures, I will turn the assignment down rather than risk my reputation by providing poor photographs in terms of both picture content and quality.
>
> I enjoy taking sports photographs and have sold many of them to *The Times Educational Supplement, Sport and Leisure* magazine and to various PR companies who are trying to promote sports goods, but I wouldn't dream of specialising in just one area. Through other areas of work, I been to 10 Downing Street, Buckingham Palace and six different countries to take photographs, as well as snapping numerous celebrities. On the hardware front, it is advisable to save and aim for a definite piece of equipment every time. I started off at college with one lens and one camera body and now I've got about £5000-worth of equipment.

Applying to a Local Paper
As with journalism, local papers are an excellent training ground but be warned – competition is very fierce and it is highly unlikely that you will be able to specialise in sport. The photographer employed by a local paper has to take everything from the town's annual flower show to the junior football team's cup tie.

To join a local paper, you should find out the addresses of, say, the ten nearest to your home, write to the editor by name explaining that you would like to join the paper and offer to show him or her some of the pictures you have already taken (your portfolio). In your portfolio you should have as wide a range of pictures as possible, neatly presented and preferably in black and white. Even if there are no vacancies at the time, the editor may suggest that you keep sending pictures on the off-chance that you've captured an event that the paper's regular photographer couldn't get to. There is then more chance of your having a picture published and this will put you in a good position when a vacancy does occur.

Chapter 9
Applying for a Job or Grant

Introduction

Everyone has to write letters of application. Even if you are a successful professional sportsman or woman, you may find yourself having to do so if, say, you are out of form and suddenly find your contract is not renewed. However talented you are, if your letter of application is badly spelt or messily presented, you may never get the chance to demonstrate those talents at an interview or a trial.

The Letter

- Prepare a rough draft of the letter first, to make sure you have covered all the essential points (age, reason for applying, why you think you would be good at the job). Mention where you saw the advertisement for the job, if applicable.
- Give details of your qualifications and past experience (your curriculum vitae) on a separate sheet of paper.
- Make sure there are no spelling mistakes or grammatical errors in your letter. If in doubt, ask a friend or teacher to look over it for you.
- Use good-quality writing paper and, if possible, have the letter typed.
- Keep your letter short and to the point; one side should be ample.
- Keep a copy of your letter for reference.

The Curriculum Vitae (CV)

See the following example for how to lay out your curriculum vitae. It should include the following information:

- Full name and address.
- Date of birth.
- Schools attended (and dates).
- Examinations passed (and dates).
- Any other honours won at school.
- Any position of authority held at school, eg school captain, soccer captain.
- Training courses, colleges or universities attended, and qualifications gained.
- Past jobs, including holiday jobs.

MARY BROWN
32 PARK AVENUE, MANCHESTER M30 5BL

Tel: 061-000 1667

DATE OF BIRTH: ————————————

AGE NOW: ——————————

SCHOOLS ATTENDED:
    (Name & town)   (From)   -   (To)

COLLEGES ATTENDED:
    (Name & town)   (From)   -   (To)

QUALIFICATIONS:
    (Name of examination)   (Subject)   (Grade)

(Include all school/college examinations which you have passed and any other qualifications/certificates you have which you think would be relevant or of interest to employers.)

POSITIONS HELD:

INTERESTS AND ACTIVITIES:

FURTHER EDUCATIONAL PLANS:

EXPERIENCE:

REFERENCES:
(1)   (Name of referee)   (Address)   (Tel no)
(2)
(3)

A sample curriculum vitae

- Present job.
- Names and addresses of two referees who can vouch for you – perhaps your PE teacher or a previous employer. Make sure these referees know you have put their names down.
- Personal interests and hobbies.
- Languages other than English.
- If you have a current driving licence, mention it.

The Interview

If your letter of application is successful, you will be asked for an interview. Here are some points to remember.

- Be on time. Even if you are five minutes late, it will count against you. So leave in plenty of time, allowing for traffic jams, slow trains, etc.
- Be smart. Even if your job is going to be one where you can wear old clothes, you will still be expected to look smart at the interview. Remember, the leisure profession is very much concerned with fitness, keenness and lack of sloppiness. Avoid 'flash' clothes, even if you feel more comfortable in them.
- Smile pleasantly and look the interviewer in the face. Speak clearly without mumbling, and do not feel you have to fill in awkward silences – that is the interviewer's job.
- Do not get angry with the interviewer or make him feel a fool by telling him that he has asked the same question twice; he is trying to find out if you can be polite and cool, even under pressure.
- Do not just answer questions with a 'yes' or a 'no' – try to add a few words of explanation. Equally, though, do not ramble – keep factual and talk about things you know and are good at; do not criticise yourself.
- Always try to appear interested in the job. Even if you are not sure you want it, look keen nevertheless; the only time you have to make a serious decision about whether you want the job is after you have been offered it!
- The interviewer will certainly ask you whether you have any questions so make sure you prepare a couple before you go in. Good ones are: 'Is there a probationary period?'; 'What are the promotion prospects?'; and 'What is the salary scale?'. Ask also about holiday entitlements, pension rights and how soon you would be required to start.
- Do *not* smoke during the interview, even if offered a cigarette. It may give an unsporting impression and present problems over ashtrays and having to keep stretching.

Checklist of Questions to be Prepared For

- ☐ What made you decide to go in for this as a career?
- ☐ What made you apply for this particular job?
- ☐ What makes you think you will be good at it?

☐ How would you like your career to develop? How does this job fit into that picture?

☐ Why do you want to leave your present job (if you already have a job)?

If you can, find someone to ask you these questions before your interview.

Accepting a Job

If you do well in your interview you will be offered the job in writing, and will be asked to accept or refuse the offer, also in writing. Before you decide, you should make sure you are clear on the following:

● What the job entails.
● What the hours, rates of pay and holiday entitlement are each year.
● How long the contract lasts for – indefinitely or for a fixed period.

Contract of Employment

A contract of employment exists as soon as someone offers you a job (even verbally) at a certain rate of pay, and you accept. Within 13 weeks of your starting work, your employer is required by law to give you written details of the contract that exists between you; these cover:

● Job title.
● Pay.
● How you are paid (weekly/monthly, by cheque/in cash).
● Hours of work.
● Holiday entitlement and pay.
● Length of notice (on both sides).
● Disciplinary and grievance procedures.
● Pension rights.
● Rules on sickness or injury absence and sick pay.

If you are not given a copy of your contract within 13 weeks of joining a firm, you should ask for it. The contract is a legal document, and you may need to refer to it later, so keep it in a safe place.

Applying for a Grant

If you are accepted for a *first-degree course* at a UK college or university or a similar course certified by the DES to be equivalent to a first degree, and have lived in Great Britain for at least three years, you should be eligible for a grant. Grants for degree students are mandatory and paid on a means-tested national scale.

In England, Wales and Northern Ireland the grant is paid by the LEA; in Scotland through the Education Department. A full grant covers tuition fees, college dues and student union fees, plus an allowance for board and lodging during term. You can also claim travelling expenses.

Full details about grants are given in the DES leaflet 'Grants for Students: A Brief Guide', available free from Department for Education, Information Division, Elizabeth House, 39 York Road, London SE1 7PH, and, for Scottish students, 'Guide to Student Allowances' from the Scottish Education Department, Awards Division, Gyleview House, Redheughs Rigg, South Gyle, Edinburgh EH12 9HH.

Discretionary grants *may* be paid by LEAs to students on *courses below degree level*. Application should be made to your local education authority on the appropriate form.

Do note, however, that a system of student loans may be introduced, to replace grants.

Part 2

Chapter 10
Sources of Information and Courses

Professional Sport

The addresses here are of the major governing bodies of the sports in Britain that are recognised and funded by the Sports Council. If in doubt about anything to do with a sport, contact the relevant governing body either by telephone or by letter. If you write, you should enclose a stamped addressed envelope: governing bodies receive many hundreds of enquires throughout the year, and have only limited finances.

Angling
National Anglers' Council
P H Tombleson, FZS – Executive Director
11 Cowgate, Peterborough, Cambridgeshire PE1 1LZ; 0733 54084

National Federation of Anglers
K E Watkins – Chief Administrative Officer
Halliday House, 2 Wilson Street, Derby DE1 1PG; 0332 362000

National Federation of Sea Anglers
D E Rowe – Development Officer
14 Bank Street, Newton Abbot, Devon TQ12 2JW; 0626 331330

Salmon and Trout Association
J H Ferguson – Director
Fishmongers' Hall, London Bridge, London EC4R 9EL; 071-283 5838

Archery
Grand National Archery Society
John Middleton – Chief Executive
The National Agricultural Centre, Stoneleigh, Kenilworth, Warwickshire CV8 2LG; 0203 696631

Association Football
Football Association
Graham Kelly – Secretary
16 Lancaster Gate, London W2 3LW; 071-262 4542

Women's Football Association
Miss L Whitehead – Secretary
448/450 Hanging Ditch, The Corn Exchange, Manchester M4 3ES; 061-832 5911

Athletics
Amateur Athletic Association
M Farrell - General Secretary
Edgbaston House, 3 Duchess Place, Hagley Road, Birmingham B16 8NM;
021-456 4050

British Amateur Athletic Board
M Farrell - Acting Secretary
Address: see Amateur Athletic Association above

Women's Amateur Athletic Association
Miss M Hartman, MBE - Secretary
Francis House, Francis Street, London SW1P 1DL; 071-828 4731

Badminton
Badminton Association of England
Geoffrey Snowdon - Chief Executive
National Badminton Centre, Bradwell Road, Loughton Lodge, Milton Keynes,
Buckinghamshire MK8 9LA; 0908 568822

Ballooning
British Balloon and Airship Club
D Davies - Secretary
PO Box 1006, Birmingham B5 5RT; 021-643 3224

Baseball
British Baseball Federation
19 Troutsdale Grove, Southcoates Lane, Hull HU9 3SD; 0482 792337

Basketball
English Basketball Association
M D Welch - Administrator
Calomax House, Lupton Avenue, Leeds LS9 7EE; 0532 496044

Bicycle Polo
Bicycle Polo Association of Great Britain
Garry Beckett - Secretary
5 Archer Road, London SE25 4JH; 081-656 9724

Billiards and Snooker
Billiards and Snooker Control Council
David Ford - Secretary
92 Kirkstall Road, Leeds LS3 1LT; 0532 440586

Bobsleigh
British Bobsleigh Association
Paul Pruszynski - Secretary
Springfield House, Woodstock Road, Coulsdon, Surrey CR3 3HS; 0737 552713

Bowls
British Crown Green Bowling Association
R Holt - Secretary
14 Leighton Avenue, Maghull, Liverpool L31 0AH; 051-526 8367

English Bowling Association
D Johnson - Secretary
Lyndhurst Road, Worthing, West Sussex BN11 2AZ; 0903 820222

English Bowling Federation
John Webb - Secretary
62 Frampton Place, Boston, Lincolnshire PE21 8EL; 0205 66201

English Bowls Council
Ray Springfield - Secretary
18 Margaret Paston Avenue, Norwich NR3 2LT; 0603 427551

English Indoor Bowling Association
B Telfer - Secretary
290a Barking Road, London E6 3BA; 081-470 1237

English Women's Bowling Association
Mrs N Colling - Secretary
Daracombe, The Clays, Market Lavington, Devizes, Wiltshire SN10 4AY;
0380 813774

English Women's Bowling Federation
Mrs I Younger - Secretary
'Irela', Holburn Crescent, Ryton, Tyne and Wear NE40 3DH; 091-413 3160

English Women's Indoor Bowling Association
Mrs P Allison - Secretary
'Jadran', 8 Oakfield Road, Carterton, Oxon OX8 3RB; 0993 841344

Boxing
Amateur Boxing Association
J H Lewis - Secretary
Francis House, Francis Street, London SW1P 1DL; 071-828 8568

Camping
Camping and Caravanning Club
G A Cubitt, MBE - Secretary
11 Lower Grosvenor Place, London SW1W 0EY; 071-828 1012

Canoeing
British Canoe Union
Paul Owen - Director
Adbolton Lane, West Bridgford, Nottingham NG2 5AS; 0602 821100

Caving
National Caving Association
Mr J Cliffe - Training Coordinator
45 Gwennyfed Avenue, Three Cocks, Brecon, Powys LD3 0RT; 0497 4575

Cricket
The Cricket Council
Alan Smith - Secretary
Lord's Cricket Ground, London NW8 8QN; 071-286 4405

National Cricket Association
Keith Andrew - Chief Executive
Lord's Cricket Ground, London NW8 8QN; 071-289 6098

Women's Cricket Association
John Featherstone - Administrative Officer
41 St Michael's Lane, Leeds LS6 3SS; 0532 742398

Croquet
The Croquet Association
B MacMillan - Administrator
Hurlingham Club, Ranelagh Gardens, London SW6 3PR; 071-736 3148

Curling
English Curling Association
R D Thornton - Secretary
66 Preston Old Road, Freckleton, Preston, Lancashire PR4 1PD; 0772 634154

Cycling
British Cycling Federation
J Hendry - Chief Executive
36 Rockingham Road, Kettering, Northamptonshire NN16 8HG; 0536 412211

British Cyclo-Cross Association
Joan Edwards - Secretary
59 Jordan Road, Sutton Coldfield, West Midlands B75 5AE; 021-308 1246

British Mountain Bike Federation
Chris Payne
36 Rockingham Road, Kettering, Northamptonshire NN16 8HG; 0536 412211

Cycle Speedway Council
R Witham - Chief Executive
57 Rectory Lane, Poringland, Norwich NR14 7SW; 0508 63880

Cyclists' Touring Club
Mr A Harlow - Secretary
Cotterell House, 69 Meadrow, Godalming, Surrey GU7 3HS; 0483 417217

Road Time Trials Council
D E Roberts - Secretary
'Dallacre', Mill Road, Yarwell, Peterborough, Cambridgeshire PE8 6PS;
0780 782464

Darts
British Darts Organisation
O A Croft - Secretary
2 Pages Lane, London N10 1PS; 081-883 5544

Fencing
Amateur Fencing Association
Miss G M Kenneally - Secretary
1 Barons Gate, 33-35 Rothschild Road, London W4 5HT; 081-742 3032

Fives
Eton Fives Association
Martin Powell - Secretary
Grafton Cottage, Bentley, Farnham, Surrey GU10 5HY

Rugby Fives Association
J F Pretlove – Secretary
1 Kennington Road, London SE1 7QR; 071-620 0383

Flying
Aircraft Owners and Pilots Association
G D Rowe – Company Secretary
50 Cambridge Street, London SW1V 4QQ; 071-834 5631

Royal Aero Club of the United Kingdom
B Rolfe – Secretary
Kimberley House, 47 Vaughan Way, Leicester LE1 4SG; 0533 531051

Gliding
British Gliding Association
B Rolfe – Secretary
Address: see Royal Aero Club of the United Kingdom above

Golf
English Golf Union
K Wright – Secretary
1–3 Upper King Street, Leicester LE1 6XF; 0533 553042

English Ladies' Golf Association
Marion Carr – Secretary
Edgbaston Golf Club, Church Road, Edgbaston, Birmingham B15 3TB;
021-456 2088

Ladies' Golf Union
Mrs A Robertson – General Administrator
The Scores, St Andrews, Fife KY16 9AT; 0334 75811

Royal and Ancient Golf Club of St Andrews
M Bonallack OBE – Secretary
St Andrews, Fife KY16 9JD; 0334 72112

Gymnastics
British Amateur Gymnastics Association
David Minnery – Secretary
Ford Hall, Lilleshall National Sports Centre, Newport, Shropshire TF10 9ND;
0952 820330

Handball
British Handball Association
Jeff Rowland – Secretary
60 Church Street, Rodcliffe, Manchester M26 8SQ; 061-724 9656

Hang-Gliding
British Hang-Gliding Association
Michael Collis
Cranfield Airfield, Cranfield, Bedford MK43 0YR; 0234 751688

Hockey
All England Women's Hockey Association
Miss T Morris – Executive Director
51 High Street, Shrewsbury SY1 1ST; 0743 233572

The Hockey Association
Stephen P Baines – Secretary
16 Northdown Street, London N1 9BG; 071-837 8878

Hovering
Hover Club of Great Britain Ltd
Mrs Brenda A Kemp – Secretary
10 Long Acre, Bingham, Nottingham NG13 8BG; 0949 37294

Ice-Hockey
British Ice-Hockey Association
David Pickles – Secretary
2nd Floor, 517 Christchurch Road, Boscombe, Bournemouth BH1 4AG;
0202 303946

Judo
British Judo Association
7a Rutland Street, Leicester LE1 1RB; 0533 559669

Korfball
British Korfball Association
G J Crafter – Secretary
PO Box 179, Maidstone, Kent ME14 1LU; 0622 813115

Lacrosse
All England Women's Lacrosse Association
Miss P Barrett – Secretary
Francis House, Francis Street, London SW1P 1DE; 071-931 8899

English Lacrosse Union
David Shuttleworth
Winton House, Winton Road, Bowdon, Altrincham, Cheshire; 061-928 9600

Land Yachting
M Hampton – Secretary
23 Piper Drive, Long Whatton, Loughborough, Leicestershire LE12 5DF;
0509 842292

Lawn Tennis
Lawn Tennis Association
J James – Secretary
Queens Club, Barons Court, West Kensington, London W14 9EG; 071-385 2366

Martial Arts
Martial Arts Commission
Mrs P Mitchell – Secretary
Broadway House, 15–16 Deptford Broadway, London SE8 4PE; 081-691 3433

Modern Pentathlon
Modern Pentathlon Association of Great Britain
Wessex House, Silchester Road, Tadley, Basingstoke, Hants RG26 6PX;
0734 810111

Motor-Cycling
Auto-Cycle Union
D G Coleman – Secretary
Miller House, Corporation Street, Rugby, Warwickshire CV21 2DN; 0788 540519

Motor-Racing
RAC Motor Sports Association Ltd
Derek Tye – Secretary
Motorsports House, Riverside Park, Colnbrook, Slough SL3 0HG; 0753 681736

Mountaineering
British Mountaineering Council
Derek Walker – Secretary
Crawford House, Precinct Centre, Booth Street East, Manchester M13 9RZ;
061-273 5835

Mountain Walking Leader Training Board
Address: see British Mountaineering Council above

Movement and Dance
The Dalcroze Society
Mrs P Pique – Secretary
26 Bullfinch Road, Selsdon Vale, South Croydon, Surrey CR2 8PW; 081-651 2889

English Amateur Dancers' Association
S Wells – Secretary
14 Oxford Street, London W1N 0HL; 071-636 0851

English Folk Dance and Song Society
John Seaborn – Administrator
Cecil Sharp House, 2 Regent's Park Road, London NW1 7AY; 071-485 2206

Keep Fit Association
Mrs Jean Jones
Francis House, Francis Street, London SW1P 1DE; 071-233 8898

Laban Art of Movement Guild
Mrs Doreen Court – Secretary
54 Priory Street, Lewes, East Sussex BN7 1HJ

Margaret Morris Movement
J Hastie – Administrator
Suite 3/4, 39 Hope Street, Glasgow G2 6AE

Medau Society of Great Britain and Northern Ireland
Mrs H Hewitt – Secretary
8b Robson House, East Street, Epsom, Surrey KT17 1HH; 03727 29056

National Association for Health and Exercise Teachers
ASSET, 112a Great Russell Street, London WC1B 3NQ; 071-580 4451

Netball
All England Association
Mrs Liz Nicholl – Director
Francis House, Francis Street, London SW1P 1DE; 071-828 2176

Orienteering
British Orienteering Federation
R Mason - Professional Officer
'Riversdale', Dale Road North, Darley Dale, Matlock, Derbyshire DE4 2HX;
0629 734042

Parachuting
British Parachute Association
Tony Butler - Secretary
5 Wharf Way, Glen Parva, Leicester LE2 9TF; 0533 785271

Paragliding
British Association of Paragliding Clubs
Mrs A Morris - Secretary
18 Talbot Lane, Leicester LE1 4LR; 0533 513007

Petanque
British Petanque Association
21 Bell Lane, Staplehurst, Tonbridge, Kent; 0580 891410

Polo
Hurlingham Polo Association
John Crisp - Secretary
Winterlake, Kirklington, Oxford OX5 3HG; 0869 50044

Rambling
The Ramblers' Association
A Mattingly - Secretary
1-5 Wandsworth Road, London SW8 2LJ; 071-582 6878

Riding
British Horse Society
C Smith - Secretary
British Equestrian Centre, Stoneleigh, Kenilworth, Warwickshire CV8 2LR;
0203 696697

British Show Jumping Association
Andrew Finding - Secretary
Address: see British Horse Society above

Roller-Hockey
National Roller-Hockey Association of Great Britain
Geoff Witte - Secretary
2 South Normandy, Warblington Street, Portsmouth, Hampshire PO1 2ES

Rounders
National Rounders Association
Brian McKinney
3 Denehurst Avenue, Nottingham NG8 5DA; 0602 785514

Rowing
Amateur Rowing Association
I W Pratt - Secretary
6 Lower Mall, London W6 9DJ; 081-748 3632

Rugby League
British Amateur Rugby League Association
H F Oldroyd - Chief Executive
West Yorkshire House, 4 New North Parade, Huddersfield, West Yorkshire
HD1 5JP; 0484 544131

The Rugby Football League
D S Oxley, MA - Secretary
180 Chapeltown Road, Leeds LS7 4HT; 0532 624637

Rugby Union
The Rugby Football Union
Dudley Wood - Secretary
Whitton Road, Twickenham, Middlesex TW1 1DZ; 081-892 8161

Women's Rugby Football Union
Meadow House, Springfield Farm, Shipston-on-Stour, Warwickshire CV36 4HQ;
0703 453371

Sailing
Royal Yachting Association
Robin Duchesne - Secretary
RYA House, Romsey Road, Eastleigh, Hampshire SO5 4YA; 0703 629962

Shooting
British Association for Shooting and Conservation
J Swift - Director
Marford Mill, Rossett, Wrexham, Clwyd LL12 0HL; 0244 570881

Clay Pigeon Shooting Association
Mr B Hammond
107 Epping New Road, Buckhurst Hill, Essex IG9 5TQ; 081-505 6221

National Rifle Association
Brigadier Peter Prescott - Secretary
Bisley Camp, Brookwood, Woking, Surrey GU24 0PB; 0483 797777

National Small-Bore Rifle Association
D King - Secretary
Lord Roberts House, Bisley Camp, Brookwood, Woking, Surrey GU24 0PB;
0483 476969

Skating
National Skating Association of Great Britain
E Waughray - Secretary
15-27 Gee Street, London EC1V 2RU; 071-253 3824

Skibob
Skibob Association of Great Britain
L G Rawson - Secretary
40 Durkar Low Lane, Wakefield, West Yorkshire

Skiing
British Ski Federation
258 Main Street, East Calder, Livingstone, West Lothian EH53 0EE; 0506 884343

Softball
National Softball Association
Stuart Houghton – General Secretary
Flat 3, 38 Netherhall Gardens, London NW3 5TP; 071-435 6781

Speedway
Speedway Control Board Ltd
John Eglese
57 Villa Crescent, Bulkington, Nuneaton CV12 9NF; 0203 643336

Squash Rackets
Squash Rackets Association
Westpoint, Warple Way, Acton, London W3 0RQ; 081-746 1616

Surfing
British Surfing Association
Colin Wilson – Secretary
T2, Champions Yard, Penzance, Cornwall; 0736 60250

Swimming
Amateur Swimming Association
D Reeves – Secretary
Harold Fern House, Derby Square, Loughborough, Leicestershire LE11 0AL;
0509 230431

Table-Tennis
English Table-Tennis Association
Robert Sinclair – Secretary
Third Floor, Queensbury House, Havelock Road, Hastings, East Sussex TN34 1HF;
0424 722525

Tchouk-Ball
British Tchouk-Ball Association
G B Osborn – Secretary
65 Shaw Green Lane, Prestbury, Gloucestershire GL52 2BS; 0452 231154

Tennis and Rackets
Tennis and Rackets Association
A Myrtle – Chief Executive
c/o The Queen's Club, Palliser Road, London W14 9EQ; 071-381 4746

Tenpin Bowling
British Tenpin Bowling Association
Mrs B Bass – Chief Executive
114 Balfour Road, Ilford, Essex IG1 4JD; 081-478 1745

Tobogganing
Great Britain Luge Association
C Dyason – Secretary
89 Tenison Road, Cambridge CB1 2DG; 0223 358438

Trampolining
British Trampoline Federation Ltd
R C Walker - Secretary
152a College Road, Harrow, Middlesex HA1 1BH; 081-863 7278

Tug-of-War
Tug-of-War Association
P J Craft - Secretary
57 Lynton Road, Chesham, Buckinghamshire HP5 2BT; 0494 783057

Underwater-Swimming
British Sub-Aqua Club
Deric Ellerby - Chairman
Telfords Quay, Ellesmere Port, South Wirral, Cheshire L65 4FY; 051-357 1951

Volleyball
English Volleyball Association
George Bulman - Director
27 South Road, West Bridgford, Nottingham NG2 7AG; 0602 816324

Water-Skiing
British Water-Ski Federation
Miss J Hill - Secretary
390 City Road, London EC1V 2QA; 071-833 2855

Weightlifting
British Amateur Weightlifters' Association
W Holland OBE - Secretary
3 Iffley Turn, Oxford OX4 4DU; 0865 778319

Windsurfing
Windsurfing Division
Royal Yachting Association, RYA House, Romsey Road, Eastleigh, Hampshire
SO5 4YA; 0703 629962

Wrestling
English Olympic Wrestling Association
Mr R Tomlinson - Secretary
16 Choir Street, Salford, Manchester M7 9ZD; 061-832 9205

Yoga
British Wheel of Yoga
Ms Jean Scales - General Secretary
1 Hamilton Place, Boston Road, Sleaford, Lincolnshire NG34 7ES; 0529 306851

PE Teaching

First Degree Courses
Two to three A levels are usually required for entrance to a first degree
course, leading to a BEd, a BSc or a BA degree. An ordinary (Ord) degree
generally lasts three years, an honours (Hons) four years. In the BEd, the
ordinary degree has been largely phased out. A Diploma of Higher
Education (DipHe) usually lasts two years and is for those not totally

committed to teaching. It is possible to transfer from it either to the third year of an academic subject degree or to the BEd. All applicants should first get a prospectus of their intended course from the college or university concerned.

Bangor Normal College
BEd (Hons) Physical and Adventure Education; 4 years, full-time

Bedford College of Higher Education
BEd (Hons) Physical Education or Dance; 4 years, full-time

BA/BSc (Hons) Sports Studies; 3 years, full-time

BA/BSc (Hons) Leisure and Recreation; 3 years, full-time

Birmingham University
BSc (Single Hons) Sport and Exercise Sciences; 3 years, full-time

BSc (Joint Hons) Sport and Exercise Sciences with either Maths, Geography or Psychology; 3 years, full-time

BA (Special Hons) Sport and Recreation Studies; 3 years, full-time

BA (Combined Hons) Sport and Recreation as 1 of 2 arts subjects; 3 years, full-time

BSocScience (Joint Hons) Sport and Recreation Studies with Sociology or Social Administration; 3 years, full-time

Bradford and Ilkley Community College
BA (Ord and Hons) Community Studies (with options in Recreational Studies); 3/4 years, full-time

Bretton Hall
BA (Hons) Dance

Brighton Polytechnic
BSc (Hons) Sports Science; 3 years, full-time

BEd (Hons) Physical Education; 4 years, full-time

Bristol University
Undergraduate certificate in Exercise and Health Studies

Cardiff Institute of Higher Education
BA (Hons) Recreation and Leisure Management; 4 years, full-time

BA (Hons) Sport and Human Movement Studies; 3 years, full-time

Charlotte Mason College of Education
BEd (Hons) Primary Education with Specialism in Outdoor and Environmental Studies; 4 years, full-time

BEd (Hons) (primary) Physical Education/Dance Studies

Chester College
BEd (Hons) Physical Education (primary); 4 years, full-time

BA (Hons) Physical Education and Sports Science; 3 years, full-time

Christ Church College
BA (Hons) Sports Science; 3 years, full-time

BEd (Hons) Sports Science; 4 years, full-time

BSc (Hons) Sports Science; 3 years, full-time

College of St Mark and St John
BEd (Hons) Physical Education (secondary) or (primary); 4 years, full-time or part-time

BA (Hons) Recreation and Community; 3 years, full-time

Crewe and Alsager College of Higher Education
BEd (Hons) (secondary) Main subjects Science or Maths. Physical Education and Outdoor Education available as supporting subjects; 4 years, full-time

BEd (Hons) (primary) Physical Education; 4 years, full-time

BSc Sports Science; 3 years, full-time

Derbyshire College of Higher Education
BEd (Hons) Human Movement Studies (including Physical Education for primary school teachers); 4 years, full-time

Durham University
BA (Ed) Physical Education; 1 year main subject, and 2 years as component of Applied Education Studies

Edge Hill College of Higher Education
BEd (Hons) Physical Education with Health Studies (primary); 4 years, full-time

BA and BSc (Hons) Degree courses which include Sports and Leisure Studies as a second subject; 3 years, full-time; 5-7 years, part-time

BA Organisation and Management Studies with option in Leisure Management; 3 years, full-time

Exeter University
BA (Ed) (Hons) Educational Studies (secondary) and Physical Education; 4 years, full-time

Glasgow University
BSc (Hons) Physiology and Sports Science; 4 years, full-time

Gwent College of Higher Education
BEd (Hons) Physical Education (primary); 4 years, full-time

Heriot Watt University
BA (Hons) Recreation; 3 or 4 years, full-time

Jordanhill College of Education
BA Sport in the Community; 3 years, full-time

BA Outdoor Education in the Community; 3 years, full-time

King Alfred's College
BEd (Hons) Human Movement Studies; 4 years, full-time

Kingston Polytechnic
BEd (Ord and Hons) Physical Education; 3/4 years, full-time

Leeds Polytechnic
BEd (Hons) Physical Education (primary); 4 years, full-time

BEd (Hons) Physical Education (secondary); 4 years, full-time

BA (Hons) Human Movement Studies; 3 years, full-time

BA (Hons) Leisure Studies; 3 years, full-time

Liverpool Institute of Higher Education
BEd (Hons) Physical Education; 4 years, full-time

BSc and BA (Hons) Physical Education in combined subjects; 3 years, full-time

Liverpool John Moores University
BEd (Hons) Physical Education; 4 years, full-time

BEd (Hons) Dance; 4 years, full-time

BEd (Hons) Outdoor and Science Education; 4 years, full-time

BSc (Hons) Sports Science; 3 years, full-time

BSc (Hons) Single Field Sports Science in combination with other subjects;
3 years, full-time

Liverpool University
BSc (Hons) Movement Science with Physical Education; 3 years, full-time

Loughborough University of Technology
BSc (Hons) Physical Education and Sports Science; 3 years, full-time

BSc (Hons) Physical Education, Sports Science and Recreation Management; 3
years, full-time

BA (Joint Hons) Physical Education, Sports Science and English; 3 years, full-time

BA (Joint Hons) Physical Education and Sports Science with Social Science, or
Physics, or Mathematics, or Chemistry or Geography; 3 years, full-time

BSc (Hons) Recreation Management

Manchester University
BA Leisure.Management; 3 years, full-time

Nene College
BA/BSc Combined Studies: Human Movement and Recreation Studies; 3 years,
full-time

BEd (Hons) Human Movement Studies (junior/infant); 4 years, full-time

Newcastle upon Tyne Polytechnic
BA (Hons) Sports Studies; 3 years, full-time

Newcastle upon Tyne University
BA (Hons) Combined Studies with a first-year option in Physical Education;
3 years, full-time

Newman and Westhill College
BEd (Hons) Physical Education (junior/infant); 4 years, full-time

North Cheshire College
BA (Hons) Leisure and Recreation; 3 years, full-time

BA (Joint Hons) Leisure and Recreation with Business Management and
Information Technology; 3 years, full-time

North East Wales Institute
BEd (Hons) Physical Education/Movement Studies (primary); 4 years, full-time

Nottingham Polytechnic
BSc (Hons) Sport (Administration and Science); 3 years, full-time

Polytechnic of North London
BEd (Hons) Health, Physical Education and Recreation (primary); 4 years, full-time

Polytechnic of West London
BA Leisure Management; 4 years, sandwich

Roehampton Institute of Higher Education
BA; BSc; (Hons) Sports Studies; 3 years, full-time

BEd (Hons) Sports Studies; 4 years, full-time

St Andrews University
BSc or MA (Ord or Hons) degree courses can include a 1-year course in Sport and Exercise Science Studies

St Mary's College
BA (Hons) with Qualified Teacher's Status in Physical Education Movement Studies (primary and secondary); 4 years, full-time

BA; BSc (Hons) Movement Studies combined with one other arts or science subject; 3 years, full-time

St Paul and St Mary's College
BEd (Hons) Physical Education; 4 years, full-time

BA (Hons) Recreations and Tourism Management; 3 years, full-time

Sheffield City Polytechnic
BA (Hons) Recreation Management; 3 years, full-time

BEd (Hons) Physical Education; 4 years, full-time

Staffordshire Polytechnic
BA (Hons) Sport and Recreation Studies; 3 years, full-time

Sunderland Polytechnic
BEd (Hons) Movement and Health Studies (primary); 4 years, full-time

BSc (Hons) Exercise and Sports Science; 3 years, full-time

Thames Polytechnic (incorporating Avery Hill College)
BEd (Hons) Movement Studies (secondary); 4 years, full-time

Trinity and All Saints' College
BA (Hons) Physical Education and Recreation with Public Media; 3 years, full-time

BA (Hons) Physical Education and Recreation (primary); 4 years, full-time

BA (Hons) Physical Education and Recreation with Business Management; Administration; 3 years, full-time

Trinity College Carmarthen
BEd (Hons) Physical Education and Outdoor Education (primary); 4 years, full-time

BA (Combined Studies) in the Rural Environment and Outdoor Education; 3 years, full-time

University College of North Wales
BA (Joint Hons) Physical Education with either Drama, Educational Studies, Linguistics, Maths or Sociology; 3 years, full-time

BA (Joint Hons) Physical Education with either French, German or Russian; 4 years, full-time

BA (Hons) Sport, Health and Physical Education; 3 years, full-time

BSc (Joint Hons) Physical Education with either Chemistry or Maths; 3 years, full-time

University College of Ripon and York St John
BA (Hons) Physical Education (Leisure Management Sports Studies/Sports Science and Dance); 3 years, full-time

University College Salford
BA (Hons) Leisure Hospitality Management Consumer Studies; 3 years, full-time (from Sept 1993)

University of Humberside
BA (Hons) Contemporary Studies: Leisure Studies Route; 3 years, full-time or 5/8 years part-time

University of Ulster at Jordanstone
BA (Hons) Sport and Leisure Studies; 3 years, full-time

BA (Hons) Sport and Leisure Studies (Sandwich course also leading to Diploma in Industrial Studies); 4 years, full-time

BA (Hons) Sport and Leisure Studies with PGCE (secondary); 4 years, full-time

Warwick University
BA (Hons) Physical Education (with Qualified Teacher Status); 4 years, full-time

West London Institute of Higher Education
BA (Hons) Sports Studies; 3 years, full-time

BSc (Hons) Sports Studies and Leisure Management; 3 years, full-time

BSc (Hons) Leisure Management; 3 years, full-time

BEd (Hons) Physical Education (secondary); 4 years, full-time

West Sussex Institute of Higher Education
BA (Hons) Sports Studies; 3 years, full-time

BEd (Hons) Secondary Physical Education; 4 years, full-time

Wolverhampton Polytechnic
BEd (Hons) Physical Education; 4 years, full-time

BA (Hons) Sports Studies; 3 years, full-time

Worcester College of Higher Education
BEd (Hons) Physical Education (primary); 4 years, full-time

BA/BSc Combined Studies (Sports Psychology); 3 years, full-time

Coaching

Not all sports have professional coaches' associations; indeed, in some sports, there are no professional coaches. If in doubt, therefore, find out from the governing body of your sport.

National Coaching Foundation
4 College Close, Beckett Park, Leeds LS6 3QH; 0532 744802

Recreation Management

There are three ways of getting into recreation management:

1. *Post-degree entry*. This ensures direct entry to the profession at managerial level.
2. *Employee entry*. This is a way of progressing from manual to managerial level.
3. *School leaver entry*. This is a means of getting a foot on the bottom rung of the recreation profession ladder. It's a long way to the top, but the structure exists to make such progress possible.

Information and advice is available from:

Institute of Baths and Recreation Management
Giffard House, 36–38 Sherrard Street, Melton Mowbray, Leicestershire LE13 1XJ; 0664 65531

Institute of Leisure and Amenity Management
ILAM House, Lower Basildon, Reading, Berkshire RG8 9NE; 0491 873558

Recreation Managers' Association of Great Britain
5 Balfour Road, Weybridge, Surrey KT13 8HE; 0932 841583

Post-degree Entry
Bangor University College of North Wales
MA/MSc/PhD; 2 years (PhD 3 years), full-time or part-time

Certificate of Further Professional Studies – Outdoor Education; 1 term

Bedford College of Higher Education
MPhil, PhD in Physical Education and Sport; 2/3 years, full-time; 3/4 years, part-time

PGCE (Physical Education or Dance); 1 year, full-time

Birmingham University
MA, MLitt, BPhil, PhD, MEd, MPhil, MSc (Exercise Sciences); 1 year, full-time; 1 or 2 years, part-time

PGCE (Physical Education)

MSoc Sci, MPhil, PhD (Leisure) by research topic agreed between candidate and institution; 1 year, full-time; 2 or 3 years according to course

Bradford and Ilkley Community College
Diploma in Management Studies (Leisure); 2 years, part-time

Outdoor Pursuits in Education and Recreation; 1 year, part-time

Brighton Polytechnic
MA (Physical Education); 2 years, part-time including 2 summer schools and 1 year, part-time for dissertation

PGCE (Physical Education or Dance); 1 year, full-time

Bristol University
PGCE (Teaching of Games second subject, Exercise and Health Studies); 1 year, full-time

Buckinghamshire College of Higher Education
Diploma in Management Studies (DMS) (Leisure and Amenity Management)

Cardiff Institution of Higher Education
MA Sport and Leisure Studies; 1 year, full-time; 3 years, part-time

Diploma in Adapted Physical Activity; 2 years, part-time

MPhil, PhD CPE, Sport Science or Leisure Studies in conjunction with University of Wales; Full-time or part-time

Charlotte Mason College
Advanced Certificate in Outdoor Education; 5 weeks, full-time

Cheltenham and Gloucester College of Higher Education
MA Tourism and Leisure; 3 semesters, full-time

Chester College
BPhil, MPhil, MEd PE and Sport Science; 2-3 years, part-time

Christ Church College
MPhil, PhD (Physical Education and Sports Studies); 4 or 6 years, part-time

Sports Science or Sports Studies; 2 or 3 years, full-time

College of St Mark and St John, Plymouth
MPhil, PhD courses in association with Cranfield Institute

Crewe and Alsager College
MSc, MPhil, PhD by Research (Physical Education); 2-6 years, part-time

Advanced Certificate in Sports Physiotherapy; 1-2 years, part-time

Advanced Certificate in Sports Podiatry; 1-2 years, part-time

Derbyshire College of Higher Education
Diploma in Education - Dance; 2 years, part-time

Exeter University
MPhil (Physical Education); 1 year, full-time; 2 years, part-time

PhD (Physical Education); 2 years, full-time; 3/4 years, part-time

PGCE (Physical Education); 1 year, full-time

Glasgow University
MEd (Physical Education and Exercise Studies); 4 years, part-time; 1 year, full-time

Advanced Diploma in Education; 1 or 2 years, part-time; or 1 year, full-time

MPhil; 2 years, part-time; 1 year, full-time

MSc (Medical Science); 2-3 years, part-time; 1 year, full-time

PhD; 5 years, part-time; 3 years, full-time

Hull University
MEd (Physical Education); 1 year, full-time; 2 years, part-time

MEd, MPhil, Phd Research Degrees in PE

MA Physical Education; 1 year, full-time

PGCE (as joint main method PE with an academic subject); 1 year, full-time

Jordanhill College
MPhil, PhD Physical Education, Sports Science, Sport and Leisure; 2 years part-time; 1 year full-time

Leeds Polytechnic
PhD or MPhil (Physical Education, Human Movement Studies or Leisure Studies); Part-time or full-time

PGCE (Physical Education); 1 year, full-time

MA Leisure and Human Potential; 1 year, full-time; 2 years, part-time

MEd (Physical Education); full-time or part-time

Leeds University
MA (Physical Education); 1 year, full-time; 2 years, part-time

Diploma in Advanced Studies in Physical Education; 9 months, full-time

Leicester University
MA/Diploma in the Sociology of Sport; 1 or 2 years full-time; 2 years, part-time; 9 months (Dip)

MSc/Diploma by distance learning in the Sociology of Sport and Sports Management; 2 years, part-time; 18 months (Diploma)

Liverpool John Moores University

PGCE (Physical Education and Dance); 1 year, full-time

Liverpool University
MSc Human Movement Science; 3 years, part-time

MPhil, PhD, (all Physical Education Movement Science); Full-time or part-time

MEd, BPhil and DASE (all Physical Education and Education); 6 years maximum, full- or part-time

PGCE (Physical Education); 1 year, full-time

MA History of Education, Physical Education Unit; 1 or 2 years, full-time; 2–4 years part-time

Loughborough University of Technology
MPhil, PhD (all Movement Sciences); 1/3 years, full- or part-time

MSc (Sports Science); 1 year, full-time

MA European Leisure Studies; 1 year, full-time

Diploma in Physical Education and Sports Science; 1 year, full-time

Manchester University
MEd (Physical Education); 1 year, full-time; 3 years, part-time

MPhil, PhD (Physical Education) Research Degrees; 1 year, full-time; 6 years, part-time

Recreation and Leisure Studies course (for qualified teachers); 1 term, full-time

PGCE (as part of primary training)
PGCE (secondary games option); 1 year, full-time

Moray House Institute, Heriot Watt University
Diploma in Recreation and Leisure Policy and Practice; 7 months, full-time; 18 months, part-time

Diploma in Professional Studies (Sports Coaching); 1 year, full-time

Diploma in Outdoor Education; 1 year, full-time

Masters (Leisure Policy and Practice) Degree; 1 year, full-time; 2 years, part-time

Newcastle upon Tyne University
Diploma in Advanced Educational Studies – PE Option; 2-5 years, part-time

MEd or MPhil; 2-5 years, part-time

PGCE Physical Education (second subject); 1 year, full-time

Newcastle Polytechnic
MSc European Master Degree in Adapted Physical Activity

North East London Polytechnic
Diploma in Management Studies (Leisure and Recreation)

Polytechnic of North London
MA (Leisure and Tourism Studies); 2/5 years, part-time

MPhil, PhD Research Degrees in Leisure, Sport and Recreation topics; 3/4 years

Diploma in Planning for Leisure; 2 years, part-time

Diploma in Management Studies (Leisure); 1 year, full-time; 2 years, part-time

St Andrews University
MSc, PhD (Physical Education or Sports Science) Research Degrees

St Paul and St Mary's College
Diploma in Recreation Studies; 2 years, full-time

Salford University
MA, MSc Modular Diploma in Advanced Studies (options in Sports Biomechanics, Perceptual-Motor Aspects of Human Performance Sports and the Arts, Exercise Physiology); 2 years, full-time

Sheffield City Polytechnic
Postgraduate Certificate in Countryside Recreation Management; 1 year, part-time

Postgraduate Diploma in Countryside Recreation Management; 2 years, part-time

MSc in Countryside Recreation Management; 1 year, full-time; 2 years, part-time

Leisure Management MSc Diploma and Certificate

Sheffield University
Leisure Management Unit
MA (Leisure Management); 1 year, full-time; 3 years, part-time

MSc Sports and Recreation Management; 1 year, full-time

Diploma in Sports and Recreation Management; 1 year, full-time

Diploma in Leisure Management; 1 year, full-time; 3 years, part-time

Dept of Physical Education and Recreation
PGCE (Physical Education); 1 year, full-time

Management School
Master of Business Administration with elective in Sport and Recreation Management; 1 year, full-time

Dept of Medical Physics and Clinical Engineering
MMed Sports and Exercise Science; 1 year, full-time; 3 years, part-time

MSc Sports Coaching; 1 year, full-time; 3 years, part-time

Southampton University
MA (Education) in PE and Curriculum Change; 1 year, full-time; 2 years, part-time

PGCE Physical Education with option in Outdoor Education; 1 year, full-time

CAES Certificate in Advanced Educational Studies in PE; 1 year, part-time

Teesside Polytechnic
Diploma in Management Studies (DMS) Leisure; 1 year, full-time; 2 years, part-time

MBA Masters in Business Administration with Leisure Management; 3 years, part-time

University College of North Wales
Certificate in Education course in Outdoor Education

University of Ulster at Jordanstown
MA (Sport and Leisure Studies); 2 years, part-time

MPhil/DPhil in Sports Studies, Sports Science or Leisure Studies by Research; Full-time or part-time

University of Warwick
MA in Sport, Culture and Society; 1 year

MA/MSc by Research; 1 year, full-time; 2 years, part-time

PhD by Research; Full-time, part-time

West London Institute of Higher Education
PGCE Physical Education (secondary); 1 year, full-time

MPhil/PhD Sports Sciences; 3 years, full-time

MSc Sport Sciences; 2 years, part-time

MSc Sport Management; 1 year, full-time

Worcester College of Higher Education
Diploma by Independent Study in Physical Education; 2 years, part-time

Certificate in PE; 1 year, part-time

PGCE Physical Education (minor course); 1 year, full-time

Worcester Technical College
Diploma in Management Studies (Leisure); 2 years, part-time

MPhil (Community PE); 3 years, part-time

Employee Entry

All these courses are organised under the auspices of the National Examination Board for Supervisory Management (NEBSM) and are usually attended by people who are already working in a swimming pool or leisure centre, but who do not as yet possess any qualification relevant to their work. Passing an NEBSM course will usually increase the successful candidate's chances of promotion. Nearly all these courses are part time; usually one day a week. As well as practical instruction, the course also involves written work.

NEBSM Courses

Capel Manor Horticultural and Environmental Centre
NEBSM Diploma in Horticulture and Recreation Management; 1 year, part-time

NEBSM Certificate in Horticulture and Recreation Management; 1 year, day-release

City of Liverpool Community College
NEBSM Certificate in Horticulture and Recreation Management; 1 year, day-release

Colchester Institute
NEBSM Recreation Management; part-time

Farnborough College of Technology
NEBSM Certificate with option in Leisure; 1 year, day-release

Harrow College of Higher Education
NEBSM Certificate in Recreation Management; 1 year, day-release

Henley College of Further Education
NEBSM Certificate in Recreation Supervision

Luton College of Higher Education
NEBSM Certificate in Supervisory Management

Matthew Boulton Technical College
NEBSM Certificate in Recreation Management; 1 year, part-time

Newark and Sherwood College
NEBSM Certificate in Recreation Management; 1 year, full-time

Newcastle College of Arts and Technology
NEBSM Certificate in Supervisory Studies (Recreation Management); 1 year, day-release

Northumberland College of Arts and Technology
NEBSM Certificate in Recreation Management; 1 year, day-release

Parson Cross College
NEBSM in Recreation Supervision; 1 year, part-time

Rochdale Technical College
NEBSM Certificate (Recreation Supervision); Part-time

St Helens College
NEBSM Diploma in Recreation Management; 1 year, part-time

NEBSM Certificate in Recreation Management; 1 year, day-release

Sandwell College
NEBSM Certificate in Leisure; 1 year, part-time

Thomas Danby College
NEBSM Certificate in Recreation Management; 1 year, day-release

Wakefield District College
NEBSM Certificate in Recreation Management; 1 year, part-time

Wigston College of Further Education
NEBSM Certificate in Supervisory Studies (Leisure Management); 1 year, part-time

Further information should be available from: National Examinations Board for Supervisory Management, 76 Portland Place, London W1N 4AA; 071-580 3050.

School-leaver Entry
BTEC courses are specially developed to prepare people for a variety of jobs in the leisure industry. They are designed to give quite a lot of choice depending on the area students want to work in, but they all include practical work experience and business and organisational studies. This means graduates can work in all areas of the leisure and tourist industry if they are unable to get a mainly sports job.

BTEC First Courses in Leisure: for students aged 16+.
No formal entry qualifications. A First Certificate takes one year, part-time and a First Diploma 1 year, full-time or 2 years, part-time.

BTEC National Courses in Leisure: for students of 16+ with a minimum of 4 GCSE passes or an appropriate First Certificate or Diploma.
A National Certificate takes 2 years, part-time and a National Diploma 2 years, full-time or 3 years, part-time.

BTEC Higher National Courses in Leisure: for students 18 and over with a relevant BTEC National award or suitable GCSE passes including one A level.
A Higher National Certificate takes 2 years, part-time and a Higher National Diploma 2 years, full-time or 3 years, part-time.

Alternative qualifications are sometimes accepted.

BTEC also runs some Continuing Education courses including special leisure courses developed in conjunction with the Institute of Leisure and Amenity Management. Some BTEC courses give some exemption from the ILAM professional level examinations.

A full list of colleges and further information should be available from:

Business and Technology Education Council
Central House, Upper Woburn Place, London WC1H 0HH; 071-413 8400.

Scottish Vocational Education Council (SCOTVEC)
22 Great King Street, Edinburgh EH3 6QH; 031-557 4555

BTEC Courses
Aberdeen College of Further Education
SCOTVEC Higher National Certificate in Leisure Management; 1 year, full-time

SCOTVEC National Certificate in Business and Leisure Studies; 1 year, full-time;
2 years, part-time

SCOTVEC National Certificate in Countryside Leisure, Recreation and Tourism;
2 years, full-time

Airedale and Wharfedale College
BTEC National Diploma in Leisure Studies; 2 years, full-time

BTEC National Certificate in Leisure Studies; 2 years, part-time

BTEC First Diploma in Leisure Studies; 1 year, full-time

BTEC First Certificate in Leisure Studies; 1 year, part-time

Aylesbury College
BTEC National Diploma in Leisure Studies; 2 years, full-time

Basford Hall College
*BTEC Continuing Education Certificate (Leisure Management); 2 years, part-
time

Basildon College of Further Education
BTEC National Diploma in Leisure Studies; 2 years, full-time

BTEC National Certificate in Leisure Studies; 2 years, full-time

BTEC First Diploma in Leisure Studies; 1 year, full-time

Bicton College of Agriculture
BTEC National Diploma in Outdoor Leisure; 2 years, full-time

BTEC First Diploma in Leisure Studies (Outdoor Pursuits); 1 year, full-time

BTEC First Diploma in Horse Studies; 1 year, full-time

BTEC Higher National Course in Business & Leisure Management

Blackpool and Fylde College of Higher Education
*BTEC Continuing Education Certificate (Leisure Management); 2 years, part-
time

Bradford and Ilkley Community College
BTEC National Certificate (Leisure Management); 2 years, part-time

BTEC National Diploma in Leisure Studies; 2 years, full-time

Buckinghamshire College
BTEC National Diploma in Leisure Studies; 2 years, full-time

BTEC National Certificate in Leisure Studies; 2 years, part-time

BTEC Higher National Diploma in Leisure Studies; 2 years, full-time

Cannington College (with Somerset College)
*BTEC Continuing Education Certificate (Leisure Management); 2 years, part-
time

---

*Courses which lead to exemption from ILAM qualifications.

BTEC First Diploma in Countryside Management; 1 year, full-time

BTEC National Diploma in Countryside Management; 2 years, full-time

BTEC First Diploma in Horse Studies; 1 year, full-time

National Certificate in the Management of Horses; 1 year, full-time

BTEC National Diploma in Horse Management with Business Studies; 2 years, full-time

BTEC HND in Golf Greenkeeping with European Studies; 3 years sandwich

Capel Manor College
*BTEC Continuing Education Certificate (Leisure Management); 2 years, part-time

Carmarthenshire Technology and Agricultural College
BTEC Higher National Certificate in Leisure Studies; 2 years, part-time

Carshalton College
BTEC National Diploma in Leisure Studies; 2 years, full-time

First Certificate in Leisure and Tourism Studies; 1 year, full-time

Castlereagh College of Further Education
BTEC First Diploma in Leisure Studies

BTEC First Certificate in Leisure Studies; 1 year, part-time

BTEC National Diploma in Leisure Studies; 2 years, full-time

*BTEC Continuing Education Certificate (Leisure Management); 2 years, part-time

BTEC Higher National Certificate in Leisure Studies; 2 years, part-time

Charles Keene College of Further Education
BTEC National Diploma in Leisure Studies; 2 years, full-time

BTEC First Diploma in Leisure Studies; 1 year, full-time

Chichester College of Technology
*BTEC Continuing Education Certificate (Leisure Management); 2 years, part-time

BTEC National Diploma in Leisure Studies; 2 years, full-time

City of Liverpool/Community College
BTEC National Diploma in Leisure Studies; 2 years, full-time

*BTEC Continuing Education Certificate (Leisure Management); 2 years, part-time

BTEC National Certificate in Leisure Studies; 2 years, part-time

BTEC National Diploma in Travel and Tourism; 2 years, full-time

Clarendon College
BTEC National Diploma in Leisure Studies; 2 years, full-time

BTEC Higher National Diploma in Leisure Studies; 2 years, full-time

BTEC National Certificate in Leisure Studies; 2 years, part-time

Colchester Institute
*BTEC Continuing Education Certificate (Leisure Management); 2 years, part-time

College of St Mark and St John
*BTEC Continuing Education Certificate (Leisure Management); 2 years, part-time

College of St Paul and St Mary
*BTEC Continuing Education Certificate (Leisure Management); 2 years, part-time

Crewe and Alsager College of Higher Education
BTEC Higher National Diploma in Business Studies/Sports Coaching; 2 years, full-time

BTEC Higher National Diploma in Sports Science; 2 years, full-time

Derby Tertiary College
BTEC National Diploma in Leisure Studies; 2 years, full-time

BTEC First Diploma in Leisure Studies; 1 year, full-time

Doncaster College
BTEC Certificate in Leisure Studies; 2 years, part-time

BTEC National Diploma in Leisure Studies; 2 years, full-time

Durham College of Agriculture and Horticulture
BTEC National Diploma in Land Use and Recreation; 3 years, sandwich course

*BTEC Higher National Diploma in Leisure Administration and Management; 2 years, full-time

East Devon College of Further Education
BTEC National Diploma in Leisure Studies; 2 years, full-time

BTEC First Diploma in Leisure Studies; 1 year, full-time

East Surrey College
BTEC National Diploma in Leisure Studies; 2 years, full-time

BTEC First Diploma in Leisure Studies; 1 year, full-time

BTEC National Certificate in Leisure Studies; 2 years, part-time

Exeter College
BTEC National Diploma in Leisure Studies; 2 years, full-time

*BTEC Continuing Education Certificate (Sport and Recreation); 2 years, part-time

Falkirk College of Technology
SCOTVEC Higher National Certificate in Leisure Management; 2 years, day-release

SCOTVEC Higher National Diploma in Leisure Management; 2 years, full-time

SCOTVEC National Certificate in Sports and Recreation Services; 2 years, full-time

SCOTVEC National Certificate in Leisure Studies; 1 year, full-time

SCOTVEC National Certificate in Sports and Recreation Services; 2 years, day-release

National Certificate in Community Sports Leadership; 2 years, part-time, 1 evening per week

Farnborough College of Technology
BTEC First Diploma in Leisure Studies; 1 year, full-time

BTEC National Diploma in Leisure Studies (also leads to College Diploma in Sports, Health and Fitness); 2 years, full-time

BTEC Higher National Diploma in Leisure Studies; 2 years, full-time; 3 years, sandwich

BTEC Higher National Diploma in the Science and Management of Health and Fitness; 2 years, full-time

*BTEC Continuing Education Certificate (Leisure Management); 1 day per week for 2 years

Fife College of Technology
SCOTVEC Higher National Diploma in Leisure Management; 2 years, full-time

SCOTVEC Higher National Certificate in Leisure Management; 1 year, full-time

Grimsby College of Technology and Arts
BTEC National Diploma in Leisure Studies; 2 years, full-time

BTEC National Certificate in Leisure Studies; 2 years, part-time

Guildford College of Technology
*BTEC Continuing Education Certificate (Leisure Management); 2 years, part-time

BTEC National Diploma in Leisure Studies; 2 years, full-time

BTEC HND in Leisure Studies; 2 years, full-time

Hammersmith and West London College
BTEC National Certificate in Leisure Studies; 2 years, part-time

Harrow College of Higher Education
*BTEC Certificate in Management Studies (Leisure); 1 year, part-time

Havering Technical College
BTEC National Diploma in Leisure Studies; 2 years, full-time

BTEC National Certificate in Leisure Studies; part-time

BTEC First Diploma in Leisure Studies; 1 year, full-time

BTEC First Certificate in Leisure Studies

Hendon College
BTEC National Diploma in Leisure Studies; 2 years, full-time

BTEC First Diploma in Leisure Studies; 1 year, full-time

Henley College of Further Education
*BTEC Continuing Education Certificate (Leisure Management); 2 years, part-time

BTEC First Diploma in Leisure Studies; 1 year, full-time

BTEC National Diploma in Leisure Studies; 2 years, full-time

BTEC National Certificate in Leisure Studies; 2 years, part-time

High Peak College
BTEC National Diploma in Leisure Studies; 2 years, full-time

*BTEC Continuing Education Certificate (Leisure Management); 2 years, part-time

Hopwood Hall College
BTEC National Diploma in Leisure Studies; 2 years, full-time

BTEC First Diploma in Leisure Studies; 1 year, full-time

BTEC National Diploma in Science (Sports Studies); 2 years, full-time

Huddersfield Polytechnic
BTEC National Diploma in Business Studies (Leisure Services option);
2 years, full-time

BTEC National Certificate in Business Studies (Leisure Services option);
2 years, part-time

Huddersfield Technical College
BTEC National Diploma; 2 years, full-time

BTEC National Certificate; 2 years, part-time

Isle College
BTEC National Diploma in Leisure Studies; 2 years, full-time

BTEC First Diploma in Leisure Studies; 1 year, full-time

Lancashire College of Agriculture and Horticulture
*BTEC Continuing Education Certificate (Leisure Management); 2 years, part-time

BTEC Higher National Diploma in Recreational Land Management; 3 years,
sandwich

Leeds Polytechnic
BTEC Higher National Diploma in Leisure Studies (Route in Recreation
Leadership available); 2 years, full-time

Longlands College of Further Education
BTEC National Diploma in Leisure Studies; 2 years, full-time

Loughborough Technical College
*BTEC Continuing Education Certificate (Leisure Management); 2 years, part-time

BTEC National Diploma in Leisure Studies; 2 years, full-time

BTEC First Diploma in Leisure Studies; 1 year, full-time

BTEC Higher National Diploma in Leisure Studies; 2 years, full-time

Luton College of Higher Education
BTEC Higher National Diploma in Business Studies (Leisure); 2 years, full-time

Matthew Boulton College
*BTEC Continuing Education Certificate (Leisure Management); 2 years, part-time

BTEC First Diploma in Leisure Studies; 1 year, full-time

Milton Keynes College
BTEC National Diploma in Recreation and Leisure Management; 2 years, full-time

BTEC First Award in Leisure Studies; 1 year, full-time

Motherwell College
SCOTVEC Higher National Diploma in Leisure Management; 2 years, full-time

SCOTVEC Higher National Certificate in Leisure Management; 1 year, full-time

SCOTVEC National Certificate in Leisure and Recreation (Sport); 1 year, full-time

Neath College
BTEC First Diploma in Leisure Studies; 1 year, full-time

BTEC National Diploma in Leisure Studies; 2 years, full-time

BTEC National Diploma in Science (Sports Studies); 2 years, full-time

BTEC National Certificate in Science (Sports Studies); 2 years, part-time

Nene College
*BTEC Certificate in Management Studies with Leisure; 1 year, part-time

Newark and Sherwood College
BTEC First Diploma in Leisure Studies; 1 year, full-time

BTEC National Diploma in Leisure Studies; 2 years, full-time

Newbury College
BTEC First Diploma in Leisure Studies; 1 year, full-time

BTEC National Diploma in Leisure Studies; 2 years, full-time

Newcastle College of Arts and Technology
BTEC National Certificate/Diploma in Leisure Studies; 2 years, full-time and part-time

New College Durham
BTEC First Diploma in Leisure Studies; 1 year, full-time

BTEC National Leisure Administration

BTEC National Sports Studies; 2 years, full-time

BTEC HND Leisure Administration; 2 years, part-time

BTEC Higher National Diploma in Leisure Studies; 2 years, full-time

North Cheshire College
*BTEC Continuing Education Certificate (Leisure Management); 2 years, part-time

BTEC National Diploma in Leisure; 2 years, full-time

BTEC First Diploma in Leisure Studies; 1 year, full-time

BTEC Higher National Diploma in Leisure Studies; 2 years, full-time; 3 years, part-time

BTEC Higher National Certificate in Leisure Studies; 2 years, part-time

North East Worcester College of Further Education
BTEC National Diploma in Leisure Studies; 2 years, full-time

BTEC First Diploma in Leisure and Recreation Studies in conjunction with CGLI 481 Parts 1 and 2; 1 year, full-time

North Lincolnshire College
BTEC National Diploma in Sport and Leisure Studies; 2 years, full-time

BTEC First Diploma in Leisure Studies; 1 year, full-time

BTEC Higher National Diploma in Sport Science; 2 years, full-time

Northumberland College of Arts and Technology
BTEC National Diploma in Leisure Studies; 2 years, full-time

BTEC National Certificate in Leisure Studies; 2 years, part-time

Norton College
BTEC National Diploma in Leisure Studies; 2 years, full-time

BTEC First Certificate in Leisure Studies; 1 year, part-time

BTEC First Diploma in Leisure Studies; 1 year, full-time

BTEC Higher National Diploma in Leisure Studies; 2 years, full-time

Norwich City College
BTEC National Diploma in Leisure Studies; 2 years, full-time

Oaklands College
BTEC National Diploma in Leisure Studies; 2 years, full-time

Oldham College of Technology
BTEC Higher National Diploma in Business Studies (Leisure); 2 years, full-time

Oxford College of Further Education
BTEC First Diploma in Leisure Studies; 1 year, part-time

BTEC First Certificate in Leisure Studies; 1 year, part-time

BTEC National Certificate in Leisure Studies; 2 years part-time

BTEC National Diploma in Leisure Studies; 2 years, full-time

Parson Cross College
BTEC National Diploma in Leisure Studies; 2 years, full-time

BTEC First Certificate in Leisure Studies; 1 year, full-time or part-time

Perth College
SCOTVEC National Certificate in Sport and Recreation; 1 year, full-time

Peterborough Regional College
*BTEC Continuing Education Certificate (Leisure Management); 2 years, part-time

BTEC National Diploma in Leisure Studies

BTEC National Certificate in Leisure Studies; 2 years, part-time

Polytechnic of North London
*BTEC Higher National Diploma in Leisure Studies; 2 years, full-time

*BTEC Certificate in Management Studies (Recreation); 1 year, part-time

Polytechnic of West London
BTEC Higher National Diploma in Leisure Studies; 3 years, sandwich

Richmond upon Thames College
BTEC Higher National Diploma in Business Studies (Leisure); 2 years, full-time

St Helens College
BTEC National Certificate in Leisure Studies; 2 years, day-release

BTEC Certificate in Management Studies – Public Sector Leisure and
Recreation; 1 year, day-release

Salford College of Technology
BTEC Higher National Diploma in Leisure Studies; 2 years, full-time

*BTEC Continuing Education Certificate (Leisure Management); 2 years, full-
time

Sandwell College of Further and Higher Education
*BTEC Certificate in Management Studies (Leisure and Recreation); 1 year,
part-time, day-release

*BTEC Continuing Education Certificate (Leisure Management); 2 years, full-
time

Somerset College of Arts and Technology
*BTEC Continuing Education Certificate (Leisure Management); 2 years, part-
time

BTEC National Diploma in Leisure Studies; 2 years, full-time

BTEC National Diploma in Leisure Management; 2 years, full-time

Southampton Institute of Higher Education
BTEC Certificate in Management Studies (Leisure and Recreation); 1 year, half-
day and evening

BTEC Higher National Diploma in Leisure Studies (Water-based Recreation); 2
years, full-time

South Devon College of Arts and Technology
BTEC National Diploma in Leisure Studies; 2 years, full-time

Southgate Technical College
BTEC National Diploma in Leisure; 2 years, full-time

BTEC First Diploma in Leisure Organisation; 1 year, full-time

Southport College
*BTEC Continuing Education Certificate (Leisure Management); 2 year, day-
release

BTEC National Diploma in Leisure Studies; 2 years, full-time

BTEC First Diploma in Leisure Studies; 1 year, full-time

Southwark College
BTEC National Diploma in Leisure Studies; 2 years, full-time

Stannington College
BTEC National Diploma in Leisure Studies; 2 years, full-time

Stockport College of Further and Higher Education
BTEC Higher National Diploma in Business Studies with Travel and Tourism
Options; 2 years, full-time

BTEC National Diploma in Leisure Studies; 2 years, full-time

BTEC National Diploma in Travel and Tourism; 2 years, full-time

BTEC First Diploma in Leisure Studies; 1 year, full-time

BTEC National Diploma in Sports Science; 2 years, full-time

Stoke on Trent College of Further and Higher Education
BTEC National Certificate in Leisure Studies; 2 years, full-time

BTEC Certificate/Diploma in Hotel, Catering, Recreation and Leisure; 2 years, full-time

Stow College
SCOTVEC Higher National Certificate in Leisure Management; 1 year, full-time; 2 years, part-time

SCOTVEC Higher National Diploma in Leisure Management; 2 years, full-time; 4 years, part-time

Sunderland University
BTEC Higher National Diploma in Leisure and Recreation (Sport and Leisure option); 2 years, full-time

Teesside University
BTEC Higher National Diploma in Business Studies (Leisure Studies option); 2 years, full-time
or HNC 2 years, part-time

Telford College of Technology
BTEC National Diploma in Leisure Studies; 2 years, full-time

BTEC National Certificate in Leisure Studies; 2 years, part-time

Thomas Danby College
*BTEC Continuing Education Certificate (Leisure Management); 2 years, part-time

BTEC National Diploma in Leisure Studies; 2 years, full-time

BTEC National Diploma in Science (Sports Studies); 2 years, full-time

BTEC National Diploma in Travel and Tourism; 2 years, full-time

BTEC National Certificate in Travel and Tourism; 2 years, part-time

BTEC National Certificate in Leisure Studies; 2 years, part-time

BTEC National Diploma in Science (Sports Studies); 2 years, full-time

BTEC National Certificate in Science (Sports Studies); 2 years, part time

BTEC National Diploma in Performing Arts; 2 years, full-time

BTEC First Diploma in Leisure Studies; 1 year, full-time

Wakefield District College
BTEC National Diploma in Leisure Studies (with A-level Sports Studies); 2 years, full-time

BTEC National Certificate in Leisure Studies; 2 years, full-time

BTEC Higher National Diploma in Leisure Studies; 2 years, full-time

BTEC First Award in Leisure Studies; 2 years, full-time

*BTEC Continuing Education Certificate (Leisure Studies); 2 years, part-time

BTEC National Diploma in Science (Sports Studies) with A-level Sports Studies; 2 years, full-time

BTEC National Certificate in Science (Sports Studies); 2 years, part-time

West Cumbria College
BTEC National Diploma in Leisure Studies with Outdoor Pursuits; 2 years, full-time

West Herts College
BTEC National Diploma in Leisure Studies; 2 years, full-time

West London Institute of Higher Education
BTEC Certificate in Leisure Management; 2 years, part-time

Wigan College of Technology
BTEC National Diploma in Leisure Studies; 2 years, full-time

Wigston College of Further Education
BTEC First Diploma in Leisure; 1 year, full-time

Diplomas and Certificates

There is now a wide range of certificate and diploma courses in sport and recreation designed for those wishing to enter the leisure industry at a junior level.

Some qualifications awarded by the colleges concerned are not validated by a national body, but most are validated by bodies such as the City and Guilds of London Institute (CGLI), the National Examination Board for Supervisory Management (NEBSM), and the Business and Technology Education Council (BTEC).

City and Guilds of London Institute

The City and Guilds of London Institute (CGLI) Certificate in Recreation and Leisure Industries (481) is intended as a qualification for those who wish to enter the leisure industry at a junior level and who wish to progress to positions of responsibility.

CGLI 481 is a four-part scheme. Each part is complete in itself:

Part 1: an introduction to the leisure industry; suitable for those who have just started work;

Part 2: will equip trainees with the skills and knowledge to work under supervision in recreation and leisure environments;

Part 3: an intermediate level suitable for those who have the ability to assist in the organisation and supervision of recreation and leisure activities;

Part 4: the final part, the Certificate in Managing Recreation and Leisure Environments, suitable for those who have the skills and knowledge required to assist in the management of leisure facilities.

Over 100 educational centres offer the courses which lead to parts 1 and 2 either in a full-time or part-time capacity. A large number also offer parts 3 and 4. A list of colleges offering the scheme can be obtained from: Section 26, City and Guilds of London Institute, 46 Britannia Street, London WC1X 9RG; 071-278 2468.

CCPR Community Sports Leaders Award Scheme

The award is non-professional and is intended for voluntary helpers of sports clubs and youth groups. It is a structured training scheme supported by the governing bodies of sport, who form an integral part of the award. Essentially a voluntary scheme with no direct job opportunities, sports leaders have been able to find employment in some sports centres; many others have been encouraged to take other sports coaching and proficiency awards to equip them for service in the leisure industry. For details please write to: CCPR Community Sports Leaders Award, Central Council for Physical Recreation, Francis House, Francis Street, London SW1P 1DE; 071-828 3163.

Certificates/Diplomas
Aylesbury College
A-level Physical Education; 2 years, full-time

Bicton College
National Certificate in the Management of Horses; 1 year, full-time

Advanced National Certificate in Equine Business Management; 1 year, full-time

Bradford and Ilkley Community College
Hanson Award; 1 year, part-time

CG DVE Sport/Recreation/Fitness Modules; 1 year, part-time

Brixton College
Certificate in Sports Coaching; 1 year, part-time

Access Sports Studies (pre-degree); 1 year, full-time

Castlereagh College of Further Education
LNCF Level 1 and selected key courses; 1 year, part-time

Charles Keene College
Certificate/Diploma in Leisure, Arts and Recreation; 1 year, full-time or part-time modules

Access Course in Sports Studies (linked to Nottingham Poly); 1 year, full-time or part-time

Advanced Course in Sports Studies – Certificate or Diploma; 2 years, full-time or part-time modules

Chichester College of Technology
PE Foundation Course with A-level Sports Studies; 2 years, full-time

CCPR Community Sports Leaders Award with BTEC and CGLI

Colchester Institute
Diploma in Leisure and Recreation Studies with CGLI 481, Parts 3 and 4 with NEBSM Recreation Management; 1 year, full-time; 1 year, part-time

Diploma in Leisure and Recreation Studies with CGLI 481, Parts 3 and 4 with GCE A levels in Sports Studies and Business Studies; 2 years, full-time

Leisure and Recreation YT (CGLI 481 Parts 1 and 2) for professional football apprentices; 2 years, full-time

Leisure and Recreation Studies (CGLI 481 Parts 1 and 2); 2 years, day-release

PE Foundation Course with CGLI 481 Part 1; 2 years, part-time

CPVE Leisure and Recreation with CGLI 481 Parts 1 and 2; 1 year, full-time

Croydon College
LTA Diploma in Tennis Management; 6 one-week blocks over 2 years

Doncaster College
Foundation Course in Sport and Recreation Studies, incorporating A-level Sports Studies; 2 years, part-time

East Devon College of Further Education
Diploma in Sport and Recreation in conjunction with A levels; 2 years, full-time

Certificate in Sport and Recreation with GCSEs; 1 year, full-time

East Surrey College
Diploma in Leisure and Recreation Studies (CGLI Part 2) (BTEC First Diploma); 2 years, full-time

Grimsby College of Technology and Arts
Sports Studies course (with CGSE and CGLI 481 Recreation and Leisure Studies, Parts 1 and 2); 1 year, full-time

Certificate in Health-Related Exercise following the YMCA syllabus; 1 year, evening course

Uniformed Services Preparatory Course (with GCSE and CGLI 481, Part 1); 1 year

Hammersmith and West London College
CPVE Services to People (Leisure)

High Peak College
CPVE Recreation and Leisure Studies; 1 year, part-time

Huddersfield Technical College
RSA Diploma Exercise to Music; 1 day a week for 12 weeks

RLSS Pool Lifeguard Bronze Medallion; 2 hours a week for 6 weeks

Isle College
Forces Preparation Course including CGLI 481 Leisure and Recreation; 1 year, full-time

Liverpool John Moores University
Diploma in Science and Football (with opportunity to gain FA coaching qualifications); 1 year, full-time

Diploma in Professional Studies (Sports Injuries and Rehabilitation, Fitness and Training); 2 terms, part-time

Longlands College of Further Education
NCFE Certificate in Exercise Studies; 1 year, part-time

Matthew Boulton College
Certificate of Competence for Sport and Recreation Operatives; 26 weeks, part-time

New College Durham
Integrated Sports Studies Combined A level/coaching/BTEC units; 1/2 years, part-time

Newbury College
Outdoor Activities Course; 2 years, full-time

Newcastle upon Tyne Polytechnic
Diploma of Higher Education Sports Studies; 1 year, full-time or part-time

Certificate of Higher Education Sports Studies; 1 year, full-time or part-time

North East Wales Institute of Higher Education
Foundation Course in Physical Education; 1 year, full-time

North Lincolnshire College
Sports Certificate (Foundation course with GCSEs – including GCSE Sports Studies); 1 year, full-time

Sports Diploma (Foundation course with A-levels Sports Studies); 2 years, full-time

RSA – Basic Certificate in the Teaching of Exercise to Music

PEA Certificate in Exercise and Health Studies

North Lindsey College
Fitness for the Forces (including CGLI 481 Parts I and II); 1 year

Leisure and Recreation Foundation (including CGLI 481 Parts I and II); 1 year

Diploma in Sport and Recreation Management (including CGLI 481 Parts III and IV and A-level PE); 2 years

GNVQ Leisure and Tourism Level 2; 1 year

GNVQ Leisure and Tourism Level 3; 2 years

Northumberland College of Arts and Technology
Sports Studies Course (with GCSE and CGLI 481 Leisure and Recreation Parts 1 and 2); 1 year, full-time or part-time

Sports Studies Course (with A levels); 2 years, full-time or part-time

Norton College
Diploma in Higher Education in Play; Full-time

CPVE Leisure Studies; Full-time

Access course to BA (Hons) Recreation and Tourism Management at Sheffield City Polytechnic; Full-time or part-time

Norwich City College of Further and Higher Education
Pre-professional College Diploma in Physical Education and Recreation Studies; 2 years, full-time

Parson Cross College
Diploma in Outdoor Education; 2 years, full-time

CPVE Leisure and Recreation; 1 year, full-time

Peterborough Regional College
Diploma in Sports Coaching; 1 or 2 years, part-time (modular)

YMCA Certificate in Health Related Fitness; Part-time

PEA Certificate in Exercise and Health Studies; 24 weeks, part-time

Pre-degree. Access to sports studies and leisure management; 1 year, part-time

Polytechnic of North London
Certificate in Physical Recreation for the Community; 1 year, part-time

Certificate in Management Studies (Recreation); 1 year, full-time

Redbridge College of Further Education
Certificate in Sports Leadership (including CGLI 481 Parts 1 and 2, GCSEs and Coaching Awards); 1 year, full-time

Redditch College
Certificate in Leisure Studies (leads to CGLI 481 Leisure and Recreation Parts 1, 2 and 3); 2 years, full-time

Richmond Upon Thames College
GCSE (AEB) Physical Education; 1 year, 6 hours per week

AEB Sports Studies Certificate of Further Studies; 1 year, 6 hours per week

Diploma of Vocational Education (Leisure); 1 year

Sandwell College of Further and Higher Education
Sports and Leisure Foundation Course; 1 year, full-time

Somerset College of Arts and Technology
A-level Sports Studies/Physical Education

Southgate College
Diploma in Sports Studies/Leisure Management/Business Studies; 2 years, full-time

Southwark College
CPVE Leisure and Amenities; 1 year, full-time

Stannington College
CPVE Recreation and Leisure Studies; 1 year, full-time

Stockport College of Further and Higher Education
Foundation Course in Sport and Recreation; 1 year, part-time

NEBSM Certificate in Supervisory Management (Recreation); 1 year, part-time

Sunderland Polytechnic – School of Social Studies
Foundation Certificate course in Stadium Crowd Management – recruitment currently only from Sunderland AFC; 20 weeks, part-time

Tameside College of Technology
Foundation Course in Physical Education; 2 years, full-time

UK Sailing Centre
Vocational Leisure Management Training Course Leading to Certificate in Management Science and Watersports Instructor's Qualifications; 12 weeks, 6 months, 1 year

University College Salford
HND in Leisure Studies (NVQ-linked); 2 years; full-time

Continuing Education Certificate in Leisure Management (NVQ-linked); 2 years, part-time

Wakefield District College
RSA Basic Certificate in the Teaching of Exercise to Music; 1 year, part-time

CPVE Leisure Studies; 1 year, full-time

West Cumbria College
College Diploma in Sport and Recreation with Outdoor Pursuits; 1 year, full-time

West Herts College
Sports and Recreation Studies with CGLI 481 Leisure and Recreation Certificate; 2 years, full-time

PEA Certificate in Exercise and Health Studies; 20 weeks, assessment

Weston-super-Mare College of Further Education
College Diploma in Physical Education with CGLI 481; 1 or 2 years, full-time

College Pre-Services Diploma with GCSE in Outdoor Education; Full-time

Wigan College of Technology
Sports Studies Foundation Course; 5 hours per week or full-time or part-time study

Leisure Studies Foundation Course; 2–6 hours per week or full-time or part-time study

Worcester College of Higher Education
Certificate in Physical Education (Primary Curriculum Leadership); Part-time modular

National Vocational Qualifications (NVQs)

NVQs and SVQs (Scottish Vocational Qualifications) are a system of vocational qualifications designed for all occupations and professions in the UK, based on the sport and leisure industry's own occupational standards. These are hallmarked by the National Council for Vocational Qualifications (NCVQ). NVQs and SVQs are based on recognising competence in particular skills required by the occupation. Therefore the qualification will be widely recognised and understood as each holder of an NVQ level will have been assessed on exactly the same units.

National standards are being prepared for six areas:

1. Coaching, teaching and instructing
2. Facility operation
3. Outdoor education, recreation and training
4. Play and play work
5. Sport development
6. Facility management.

NVQs were introduced on 1 April 1992. However, they are not fully formed or compulsory. Pilot schemes are taking place at present and the first people to progress through all the levels will take five years from 1992. Therefore, do not panic if you already hold qualifications. The best thing to do is to keep a portfolio of experience and contact your governing body, or NCVQ direct, whose address is: National Council for Vocational Qualifications, 222 Euston Road, London NW1 2BZ; 071-387 9898.

A Levels

The GCSE Advanced level syllabus in Sports Studies is available at 66 colleges of further education. The GCSE Advanced level syllabus in Physical Education is offered as part of a limited pilot scheme at 12 colleges.

Details of colleges offering these courses can be obtained from: The Associated Examining Board, Stag Hill House, Guildford, Surrey GU2 5XJ; 0483 506506.

Sports Scholarships

Sports scholarships are available at the following universities:

University of Bath
Department of Sport and Physical Recreation, Claverton Down, Bath BA27 7AY; 0225 826826

University of Newcastle
Newcastle upon Tyne, Tyne and Wear NE1 7RU; 091-222 6000

University of Oxford
The Richard Blackwell Scholarship Trust, St Catherine's College, Oxford OX1 3UJ; 0865 271700

University of St Andrews (Golf)
College Gate, St Andrews, Fife KY16 9AJ; 0334 76161

University of Salford
The Crescent, Salford, Lancashire M5 4WT; 061-745 5000

University of Stirling
Stirling, Stirlingshire, Scotland FK9 4LA; 0786 73171

University College of Swansea
Singleton Park, Swansea SA2 8PP; 0792 205678; and at Lansdowne College, 7-9 Palace Gate, London W8 5LS; 071-581 3307 (A levels)

Institute of Leisure and Amenity Management

ILAM is a professional institute for leisure and recreation managers in the public and private sectors. ILAM runs its own professional examinations, but courses relating to the ILAM Certificate and Diploma qualifications are validated either by BTEC or CNAA, not directly by ILAM. Such courses (eg BTEC Continuing Education Certificate in Leisure Management or CNAA Diploma in Management Studies (Leisure)) will give substantial exemptions from ILAM examinations.

See the sections on BTEC courses and postgraduate courses for relevant courses.

Institute of Baths and Recreation Management

The IBRM is primarily a qualifying institution for managers in swimming pools and sports and leisure centres operated by local authorities. Obtaining the Institute's qualification includes a two-year period of study to prepare for the Membership (intermediate) examination. For those who wish to enhance their career by obtaining the Diploma (Final) qualification, a further period of study of at least one year is required in preparation for the examination. (IBRM's address is given on page 108.)

Courses are offered at the following colleges:

Airedale and Wharfedale College
Calverley Lane, Horsforth, Leeds LS18 4RQ; 0532 581723

Blackpool and Fylde College of Further and Higher Education
Ashfield Road, Bispham, Blackpool FY2 0HB; 0253 52352

Cardiff Institute of Higher Education
Cyncoed Centre, Cyncoed Road, Cyncoed, Cardiff CF2 6XD; 0222 551111

City of Liverpool Community College
Bankfield Road, Liverpool L13 0BQ; 051-259 1124

Clarendon College
Felham Avenue, Mansfield Road, Nottingham NH5 1AL

Henley College
Henley Road, Bell Green, Coventry CV2 1ED; 0203 611021

Huddersfield Technical College
New North Road, Huddersfield, West Yorkshire HD1 5NN; 0484 536521

James Watt College
Finnart Street, Greenock, Inverclyde PA16 9AJ; 0475 24433

Lewisham London College
Department of Construction, Worsley Bridge Road, London SE26 5BD; 081-650 8227

Longlands College of Further Education
Douglas Street, Middlesborough, Cleveland TS4 2JW; 0642 248351

Matthew Boulton College
Sherlock Street, Birmingham B5 7DB; 021-440 2681

Milton Keynes College
Chaffron Way, Milton Keynes, Buckinghamshire MK6 5LP; 0908 668998

North Lincolnshire College
Cathedral Street, Lincoln LN2 5HQ; 0522 510530

North Lindsey College
Kingsway, Scunthorpe, South Humberside DN17 1AJ; 0724 281111

Norton College
Dyche Lane, Sheffield S8 8BR; 0742 372741

Parsons Cross College
Remington Drive, Sheffield S5 9RB; 0742 736273

South Fields College of Further Education
Aylestone Road, Leicester LE2 7LW; 0533 541818

South Nottingham College of Further Education
Greythorn Drive, West Bridgford, Nottingham NG2 7GA; 0602 812125

Stoke on Trent College of Further Education
The Concourse, Stoke Road, Sheldon, Stoke on Trent, Staffordshire ST4 2DG;
0782 208208

Wirral Metropolitan College
Borough Road, Birkenhead, Merseyside L41 6NH; 051-653 5555

Candidates enrolling on these courses must be in full-time employment in the
baths and recreation service.

Correspondence Courses

The National Association of Local Government Officers (NALGO) Education courses are conducted via correspondence, and represent the only
distance-learning route to these qualifications. It is not necessary to be a
NALGO member. The following courses are available:

> ILAM Certificate – 1 year approx
> IBRM Membership (Intermediate) – 2 years approx
> IBRM Diploma (Final) – 1 year approx

For further information, contact: NALGO Education, 1 Mabledon Place,
London WC1H 9AJ; 071-388 2366, ext 435

Professional Associations

British Association of National Sports Administrators
Mrs R Hallam – Secretary
c/o Scottish Amateur Swimming Association, Airthrey Castle, University of
Stirling, Stirling FK9 4LA

British Sports and Allied Industries Federation Ltd
L Standen – Chief Executive
23 Brighton Road, South Croydon, Surrey CR2 6EA; 081-681 1242

Chief Leisure Officers' Association
E L Harris – Hon Secretary
Stevenage Borough Council, Daneshill House, Danestrete, Stevenage,
Hertfordshire SG1 1HN; 0438 356177, ext 234

Institute of Baths and Recreation Management
G May
Giffard House, 36–38 Sherrard Street, Melton Mowbray, Leicestershire
LE13 1XJ; 0664 65531

Institute of Groundsmanship
W D Walder – Hon General Secretary
19–23 Church Street, The Agora, Wolverton, Milton Keynes MK12 5LG; 0908
312511

Institute of Leisure and Amenity Management
Alan Smith - Director
ILAM House, Lower Basildon, Reading, Berkshire RG8 9NE; 0491 873558

Recreation Managers' Association of Great Britain
Mrs E H Clarke - Administration Officer
5 Balfour Road, Weybridge, Surrey KT13 8HE; 0932 841583

Chapter 11

Useful Addresses

The Sports Council

The Sports Council has its head office at 16 Upper Woburn Place, London WC1H 0QP; 071-388 1277; it also has nine regional offices in England. Contact the one in your area for details of local sports events and organisations.

Northern Region (Northumberland, Cumbria, Durham, Cleveland, Tyne and Wear)
Aykley Heads, Durham DH1 5UU; 091-384 9595

North West Region (Lancashire, Cheshire, Greater Manchester and Merseyside)
Astley House, Quay Street, Manchester M3 4AE; 061-834 0338

Yorkshire and Humberside Region (West, South and North Yorkshire, Humberside)
Coronet House, Queen Street, Leeds LS1 4PW; 0532 436443

East Midland Region (Derbyshire, Nottinghamshire, Lincolnshire, Leicestershire, Northamptonshire)
Grove House, Bridgford Road, West Bridgford, Nottingham NG2 6AP; 0602 821887/822586

West Midlands Region (Metropolitan County Council of West Midlands, Hereford and Worcester, Shropshire, Staffordshire and Warwickshire)
1 Hagley Road, Five Ways, Birmingham B16 8TT; 021-456 3444

Eastern Region (Norfolk, Cambridgeshire, Suffolk, Bedfordshire, Hertfordshire, Essex)
Crescent House, 19 The Crescent, Bedford MK40 2RT; 0234 345222

Greater London and South-East Regions (Greater London, Surrey, Kent, East and West Sussex)
PO Box 480, Crystal Palace National Sports Centre, Ledrington Road, London SE19 2BQ; 081-778 8600

Southern Region (Hampshire, Isle of Wight, Berkshire, Buckinghamshire, Oxfordshire)
51a Church Street, Caversham, Reading, Berkshire; 0734 483311

South-West Region (Avon, Cornwall, Devon, Dorset, Somerset, Wiltshire, Gloucestershire)
Ashlands House, Ashlands, Crewkerne, Somerset TA18 7LQ; 0460 73491

Offices of the Sports Council in Scotland, Northern Ireland and Wales are:

The Scottish Sports Council
Caledonia House, South Gyle, Edinburgh EH12 9DQ; 031-317 7200

The Sports Council for Northern Ireland
The House of Sport, 2a Upper Malone Road, Belfast BT9 5LA; 0232 381222

The Sports Council for Wales
National Sports Centre, Sophia Gardens, Cardiff CF1 9SW; 0222 397571

Other Organisations

Association of Playing Fields Officers
K E Hill - General Secretary
1 Cowley Road, Tuffley, Gloucestershire GL4 0HT; 0452 425355

British Blind Sport
Ian Fell - Secretary
Heygates Lodge, Elkington, Northampton NN6 7NH; 0858 575584

British Council of Physical Education
F Hirst - Secretary
PO Box 6, Woolton Road, Liverpool L16 8ND; 051-722 7331

British Deaf Sports Council
R Haythornwaite - Administrator
7a Bridge Street, Otley, West Yorkshire LS21 1BQ; 0943 462917

British Sports Association for the Disabled
Caroline Bradley - Chief Executive
The Mary Glen Haig Suite, Solecast House, 13-27 Brunswick Place, London
N1 6DX; 071-490 4919

Central Council of Physical Recreation
P Lawson - General Secretary
Francis House, Francis Street, London SW1P 1DE; 071-828 3163

Health Education Authority
Dr S Hagard - Director General
Hamilton House, Mabledon Place, London WC1H 9TX; 071-631 0930

National Association for Outdoor Education
Barbara Humberstone
251 Woodlands Road, Woodlands, Southampton SO4 2GS; 0703 292546

National Coaching Foundation
4 College Close, Beckett Park, Leeds LS6 3QH; 0532 744802

Sports Aid Foundation
Brigadier Noel Nagle - Director
16 Upper Woburn Place, London WC1H 0QN; 071-387 9380

Sports Documentation Centre
Main Library, University of Birmingham, PO Box 363, Birmingham B15 2TT;
021-414 5843 ext 2312

Universities Central Council on Admissions (UCCA)
PO Box 28, Cheltenham, Gloucestershire GL50 1HY; 0242 222444